THINKING IN STORY

Preaching In A Post-literate Age

BY RICHARD A. JENSEN

C.S.S. Publishing Co., Inc.
Lima, Ohio

THINKING IN STORY

Copyright © 1993 by
The C.S.S. Publishing Company, Inc.
Lima, Ohio

Reprinted 1994

Scripture quotations are from the *New Revised Standard Version of the Bible,* copyright 1989 by the Division of Christian Education of the National Council of the Churches of Christ in the USA. Used by permission.

Library of Congress Cataloging-in-Publication Data

Jensen, Richard A.
    Thinking in story : preaching in a post-literate age / by Richard A. Jensen.
    145 p.   14 by 21.5 cm.
    Includes bibliographical references.
    ISBN 1-55673-573-1
    1. Preaching. 2. Storytelling — Religious aspects — Christianity. I. Title
BV 4235.S76J46   1993
251—dc20

              92-38127
              CIP

9319 / ISBN 1-55673-573-1   PRINTED IN U.S.A.

THINKING
IN STORY
Preaching In A
Post-literate Age

Table Of Contents

Preface

It has been a decade plus since my initial work on preaching, *Telling The Story,* made its appearance. At the time I wrote that book I was working in Systematic Theology. *Telling The Story* was the reflection of a theologian on the task of preaching. I had begun to see then that communication media had a powerful impact on preaching. In *Telling The Story* I explored, for example, how the rise of print through the invention of the printing press gave shape to a new form of preaching. Gutenberg hermeneutics, I proposed, created Gutenberg homiletics. Gutenberg homiletics, I suggested, predisposes a didactic form of homiletics. The linear massage of print helped to create a linear approach to the task of proclamation. The characteristics of "Gutenberg homiletics" are as follows:

- the goal of preaching is to teach the lessons of the text.
- in order to teach the lessons or meaning of the text, the points to be made are usually abstracted from the text.
- the sermon is aimed primarily at the hearer's mind.
- the sermon is developed in a logical, sequential and linear manner.
- the sermon is prepared under the criteria for written material.
- the faith engendered in the hearer is "faith" that the ideas are true.[1]

Telling The Story explored this didactic form of preaching that was in many ways a product of the medium of print and then went on to talk about other ways to envisage the preaching task. "Proclamatory" preaching and "Story" preaching were proposed as alternatives to the didactic straightjacket that enslaved too much of the homiletical enterprise.

Thinking In Story is in many ways an extension of *Telling The Story.* I write today not as a practitioner in the field of systematic theology but as a preacher who is heavily involved in the mass media of radio and television. For the past 10 years I have prepared weekly sermons for a nationwide radio broadcast called Lutheran Vespers. During this same course of time I have helped to produce several short series of television programs. For the past 10 years, in other words, I have been immersed in the mass media. I have gained a much greater depth of understanding of mass media in these years. I have done much research in the field of oral communication, the era prior to print. I have come to understand much more clearly how the contemporary media of radio and television impact their listeners. I am particularly concerned with the era of mass media in which we live. How shall we preach to a people whose lives are mightily shaped by the sounds and the visual images that impact their lives with unrelenting power?

Nearly all the experts in communication agree that the world has experienced three communication eras. The first era was an era of oral communication; the second began with writing and continued with print; the third is the era of electronic communication which is now coming to birth. The unique reality of our generation is that we are living on the forefront of a shift from one communication era to another. We are living on the boundary between the print era and the electronic era. We must understand, therefore, that we are living through revolutionary times. A shift in communication media has occurred only once before in human history. That was the shift from oral communication to print and written communication. Today we move from the world of print to the world of electronics. This is a revolution. It is a revolution that calls upon us to seriously re-think most of what we do. It is certainly a revolution that calls us to reinvestigate preaching in our time.

In Chapter One I begin this exploration by seeking to understand how communication culture effected preaching design in previous eras. I attempt to show how preaching might have been shaped in the era of oral communication and contrast that with the way preaching has been shaped by written and print communication. One of the basic differences in preaching design that I suggest is that the preacher in an oral culture thinks in stories while the preacher in a literate culture thinks in ideas. It is from this contrast that I take the title for my work.

Chapter Two looks at our post-literate age and seeks to understand how preaching might be reshaped in our time. Communication experts are generally in agreement that there is much about our post-literate culture which is like early oral culture. Walter Ong, for example, calls our era a "secondary oral" era. Primarily we are talking here about the return of sound with radio and television. The ear is put back to work. A strictly literate era needs no ear; only eyes. I suggest, therefore, that we can learn much about preaching in our time from the earliest oral era of human communication. People in those cultures thought in stories. Thinking in stories is one way that we can structure sermons for people in a post-literate world. In a sense we go "back to the future." The thinking mode of oral cultures of long ago holds some possibilities for our preaching in an electronic culture.

Chapter Three takes a break from the flow of material in order to discuss theology and preaching. Before turning to the practical matter of how to "think in story," I felt it necessary to spend some time on the subject matter of preaching. I do this by joining a conversation with several recent and pivotal works that relate to theology and preaching. In my estimation, theology of preaching is not attended to with enough seriousness within the homiletical establishment. This is why I feel I must address the subject, if briefly, in seeking to give shape to preaching in our time. Chapters One and Two seek to lay out the form preaching might take in our era. Chapter One and Two, therefore, set forth the theory behind certain forms of preaching. Chapter Three deals with the content of preaching.

Chapters Four and Five are practical chapters. Chapter Four explores the sources of stories. If we are to learn to "think in stories" what are the sources of such stories? Chapter Five deals with a variety of ways of structuring our stories into completed sermons. Chapter Six explores some of the problems and limitations of the story approach to preaching. Chapter Six briefly explores alternative ways to communicate the gospel in a post-literate world.

In a decade of thought about preaching, therefore, I have moved from advice for "telling the story" as a way of preaching to advocating story as a way of thought: "thinking in story." I trust you will catch the full strength of this shift. I am seriously proposing a kind of paradigm shift for preachers shaped by the literate world's approach to preaching. One of the ways we can communicate the gospel in our time is by learning a new thought process. We have learned to think in ideas. We have learned to preach sermons that were primarily filled with ideas. Now we must also learn how to think in stories. This is a different way of thinking that commends itself most highly in seeking to be effective communicators of the gospel in these times of communication revolution.

It is clear that my work will strongly advocate the story or narrative approach to preaching. There are any number of works in the area of homiletics today that urge narrative preaching. I see my contribution to this field as supplying an overarching framework for the use of story. I try to ground the use of story in an understanding of communication eras. My contribution is also in the form of demanding a new form of thinking. We are not simply to tell stories. We must learn to think in stories. That is one of the keys, I believe, to effective preaching in our time.

I advocate the use of "story thinking" in the face of both a theoretical and popular reaction to story as the way of preaching. I think the scholarly reaction to narrative preaching is beneficial for us all. I hope that this work will contribute to a healthy dialogue about preaching. Pastors who preach each week are well served by a strong dialogue on the nature of the task.

There is also a popular backlash against preachers and their stories. I hear it all the time. "I'm tired of all these stories. I don't get the point. All the preacher does is tell stories." It is imperative that we take this reaction seriously. My own impression is that the complaints people have are complaints about the loss of the Bible in this flurry of stories. I want to state with all the strength of my being that sermons think in stories and tell stories in the service of biblical texts. We don't tell stories to entertain, to make things more interesting or to lighten up the preaching task for people. We tell stories in order that the Bible might come alive for people in ever new ways. In fact, as I will suggest, many of the stories we will tell are Bible stories! I am absolutely convinced that as long as people see that our stories enliven scripture they will not protest the story form. It is absolutely mandatory that the preacher/storyteller tell his or her stories for the sake of the greatest story ever told.

I have been working out the shape of this material over the course of the past several years. I have shared this material in different forms with many pastoral groups. The response of pastors has constantly helped me sharpen my focus, change things that are of dubious worth and add things which one only learns in the give and take with many listeners. I have also taught this material at undergraduate and graduate levels at the Lutheran School of Theology at Chicago, and Pacific Lutheran Theological Seminary. I owe a strong debt of gratitude to my many students for their patience and participation. I must say that the strongest case I can make for the method of preaching I propose here is the sermons I have heard by students in these classes. Having heard their sermons I am emboldened to share this approach with a wider audience. I thank them one and all.

Preaching is a high and holy calling. The preacher is given the awesome opportunity to proclaim the good news of God's love for sinful humanity in Jesus Christ. It is my prayer that some of what I have written here helps you fulfill the high and holy call to preaching that comes from God.

----

1. Richard A. Jensen, *Telling The Story: Variety and Imagination in Preaching,* (Minneapolis, Augsburg, 1980), p. 27.

Foreword

At first blush, it is remarkable that a professional systematic theologian has written a book on thinking in story. One would not normally expect a theologian to propose that we learn to think in categories other than theological ideas. But that is precisely what Richard Jensen is proposing. Who would have predicted that a Reformation theologian would take such a step?

Jensen's proposal emerges out of a growing recognition of the situation of the church in the late 20th century. In this electronic age, the church faces a new communications challenge: how is the gospel of Jesus Christ to be proclaimed and made meaningful in a culture that no longer values literacy and its modes of thought as the most advanced means of communication? This is the first period in the history of Christianity in which the most powerful medium of cultural communication is not writing. From a communications perspective, therefore, we live in the period of the greatest change since the formation of the church.

It is no surprise from this perspective that there is a crisis in the theory and practice of preaching. If styles of preaching that were powerful for the communication of the gospel in one culture were used in a radically different culture, we would not be surprised if they did not communicate. But, because we are immersed in electronic culture, we often do not recognize the radicality of its differences from literate culture and are surprised when our literate preaching does not communicate in this new cultural age. The first step, therefore, in addressing this new situation is to recognize the relationship between strategies for preaching and communications culture.

But the far more difficult step is to develop a new way. If it is true that our religious tradition has been formed for almost 2000 years by the communication culture of literacy, how can we get enough distance from it to think about an

13

alternative? The proposal of this book is that we look back to the preliterate, oral stage of the tradition for a clue. In the Bible, we have a record of the sounds of the oral traditions of Israel. And those traditions have a striking characteristic: more than half of both the Old and New Testament are stories. The formation and telling of stories was the most formative communications tradition in the religion of Israel. Equally striking is that the forms of doctrinal argument that have had such a major role in the Christian tradition are virtually nonexistent in the canonical literature. In fact, the characteristic forms of doctrinal argument were a largely post-biblical development. In the biblical tradition, the storytellers were the most powerful thinkers.

This book is part of a broad communal intuition that narrative has a uniquely central role in the future of Christianity. This awareness has emerged within the last 20 years in a variety of forms. In biblical studies, there has been a multi-faceted movement to exegete and interpret biblical narratives as narratives rather than as theological illustrations. In theology, the development of narrative theology has been an effort to rethink the role of narrative in Christian thought and practice. In pastoral care and Christian education, new modes of spiritual direction and curriculum development have emerged from a reinvestigation of the role of story in spiritual formation and in learning. And in preaching, narrative preaching has become such a widespread interest that it is already being dismissed as a fad.

If this analysis is correct, narrative preaching is not a fad but is a response to a deep and pervasive need at the core of the issues facing the church. The need is to develop ways of thinking and communicating that will be faithful and effective in the electronic age. In effect, it is a new manifestation of the steady need to reinvestigate the relationship between scripture and tradition as a primary means for the reformation of our minds for the proclamation of the gospel in new cultural contexts. The proposal here is at the core of such a reformation: we need to learn to think in story.

Of course, we cannot go back to an oral culture and its modes of thought. We will not think in story in the same ways as ancient storytellers. Nor is it any surprise that there have been false starts and a number of relatively superficial efforts at narrative preaching that have rightly been criticized as "mere" entertainment. But such a critique can hardly be appropriate for the notion of thinking in story. Can one imagine criticizing the stories of the Yahwist, Deuteronomist, Luke and John as superficial and merely entertaining communication? However, a pervasive and profound reappropriation of narrative modes of thought will take a long time to be formed. Only then will we know whether or not learning to think in story has helped the church form patterns of communication that connect with the mind of the electronic global culture. In the meantime, maybe it isn't such a surprise that a reformation theologian should be one who is taking first steps in calling the church to a new reformation.

Thomas E. Boomershine
Professor of New Testament
United Theological Seminary
Dayton, Ohio

CHAPTER ONE
Communication Cultures And Preaching Design

According to experts in communication theory the human race has lived in three communication eras. As Walter Ong puts it: ". . . it has become evident . . . in terms of communications media, (that) cultures can be divided conveniently and informatively into three successive stages: (1) oral or oral-aural (2) script, which reaches critical breakthroughs with the invention first of the alphabet and then later of alphabetic movable type, and (3) electronic . . . these three stages are essentially stages of verbalization. Above all they mark transformations of the word."[1]

The biblical word of God has been preached in each of these communication eras of Western culture. Biblical preaching in these succeeding eras is powerfully shaped by the communication culture in which it lives. Preaching in an oral-aural culture differs markedly from preaching in the era of writing and print, for example. Communication cultures change very rarely in human history. As we have heard from Walter Ong, and nearly all scholars in the communications field agree with his demarcations, there have really only been two major shifts in communication culture in the entire history of humankind. We stand today at the beginning of the second major shifting of the eras. We stand today at the transition between print and electronic, literate and post-literate, cultures. This means that the task of preaching must be reexamined in our day. Preaching in an electronic culture will be quite different from preaching shaped in the previous communications culture of print. Before we can propose what form preaching might take in this new era we need to understand more fully how the task of preaching was impacted in the past by the communications culture in which it lived. Examining the morphology of preaching up until this era of change is the task of this chapter.

Preaching In An Oral-Aural Culture

The primary form of communication in an oral-aural culture was the human voice. In an oral culture the word is something that happens, an event in the world of sound. The ear, on the other hand, is the sensory apparatus that receives the communication. Marshall McLuhan taught us that the medium is not only the message; the medium is also the massage. McLuhan believed that the way we receive information (the massage) is as important as the message itself. In an oral-aural world it is the ear that is massaged. The fact that the ear is the primary receiving sense shapes the nature of oratory, the nature of preaching, that can be received by the ear.

The word is an event in the world of sound. This stands in contrast to a word in the writing culture which will follow where a word lives in space. Word as sound has several characteristics. Sound is more real or existential than other sense objects. Sound alone is related to present actuality rather than to the past or future. Sound penetrates being. It comes out of the interior of one person and reaches the interior of another person. Sound, therefore, may be a physical means of God's presence to us just as water and bread and wine in the sacraments are physical signs of God's presence. The preached word enters peoples bodies!

Where the sounded word is received by the listener there is always community. It takes two to sound! Sound situates us in human community in contrast to later print culture which makes it possible to learn in isolation from other people. Print is the technology of individualism. With sound we are placed in the middle of a world and in simultaneity. Vision, on the other hand, puts us in front of things and in sequentiality.[2]

It is only in recent times that scholars have discovered the dynamics of oral cultures. "Oral literature" that has been handed down to us from antiquity has traditionally been studied in the same way as we study literature from the world of writing and print. Breakthroughs into the dynamics of oral literature came first with studies of Homer by Milman Parry during the first third of this century. Parry discovered that Homer's poetry was shaped completely by orality and not by literary canons. Oral tellers of tales rhapsodized. According to *Webster's New World Dictionary* our word rhapsody comes from two Greek words: *rhaptein* which means one who strings songs together, and *oide* which means song. To rhapsodize, therefore, is to stitch songs/stories together.

The storyteller ". . . dips into a grab bag of phrases and adjectives and, driven by the rhythms of the lyre, spins the yarn of a tale. . . . The lines of the *Iliad* do not consist of a series of words. Those who sang it were driven by the rhythm of the lyre. . . . Homer sang as a prehistoric rhapsode. . . . Homer's art consisted of stitching together a series of stock words and phrases."[3]

The philosopher, Plato, stood at the bridge between oral and written culture. "Plato was not Greece's first author. But he was the first uneasy man of letters. He was the first to write with the conviction of the superiority of thought unrelated to writing."[4] In his monumental work, *The Republic,* Plato excluded oral poets from his ideal world ruled by philosopher kings. Walter Ong refers to this as the first media clash in human history. "Plato's exclusion of poets from his *Republic* was in fact Plato's rejection of the pristine aggregative, paratactic oral style thinking perpetuated by Homer in favor of the keen analysis or dissection of the world and of thought made possible by the interiorization of the alphabet in the Greek psyche."[5]

In *Orality and Literacy,* Walter Ong gives a detailed description of the psycho-dynamics of oral culture.[6] I will share a brief summary of these psycho-dynamics and refer you to Ong's work for further study. Ong indicates, first of all, that sounded words have power and action. This world of sound is often referred to as a "magical world of sound." "The interiorization of the technology of the phonetic alphabet translates man [sic] from the magical world of the ear to the neutral visual world."[7]

I witnessed this accent on sound as a missionary in Ethiopia when I came to understand something of the oral precision of the liturgy of the Ethiopian Orthodox Church. Until very recently the priests in the Orthodox Church received a rather simple training. What they learned most of all was how to recite the liturgy perfectly. The illiterate worshiper expected a certain sound and that sound could not be changed. We experience this in our time, perhaps, when we read stories to children. They want the same sounds; they don't want us to improvise. Sound has power!

Secondly, in an oral world one only knew what one could recall. Knowledge was limited by memory. A speaker in this culture had to have memnonic devices built into his/her rhapsodizing so that the hearer would later remember the content.

Thirdly, the structure of sentences is quite simple. Rarely is there a subordinative clause. Sentences are just added to each other. We can observe this simple adding together of sentences in many of the narrative portions of scripture. Sentences are simply linked with the word and. In an earlier work I proposed what I called "Jensen's First Law of a Boring Sermon." This law refers to the fact that when we are bored by a sermon we ought to first check out the length of the sentences. Usually we will discover that the sentences are very long. What I understand better at this juncture is that the length of the sentence is not necessarily the problem. The problem lies with sentences that are composed under the canons of print, sentences that work wonderfully well for the eye. They do not work well for ears, however.[8]

A fourth characteristic of oral cultures in terms of communication is that the teller of the tale relies heavily on stock words and phrases that can be shaped and reshaped to the beat of the music. The rhapsodizer composed out loud by improvisation. They composed and recited in the same moment.

A fifth characteristic is redundancy. The rhapsodizer repeated some phrases over and over again. This is an aid to memory. Written communication gives a sense of continuity outside of the mind. Our eyes can always review the page for data we have forgotten. Not so in an oral culture. The auditor relied heavily on the redundant character of the story/song in order to be able to remember what was said/sung.

Sixth, oral cultures repeat the traditions of their people many times over. It is only in the telling of the tale that the tradition of the people can be kept alive. The storyteller, therefore, helps to conserve tradition.

Next, the tone of the story was often a tone of conflict. There was a strong polemic in the storytelling of pre-literate peoples. This story, after all, is the story that legitimizes this community over and against other communities. The stories, therefore, are filled with heros. The hero of the epic embodies the values of the people. I am convinced that much of this tone of conflict remains in the life of Martin Luther. Luther, like Plato, lived at the junction of communication worlds. In Luther's case it was the junction of a culture still oral in much of its tone though it was filled with manuscript writing and stood on the brink of the new world of the printing press. The oral world was still lived in Luther. His polemical attitude is typical of the culture of oral communications.

Eighth, we are to understand that storytellers in the oral world lived in empathy with the world around them. When

21

writing came along the knower and the known became separated. One wrote objectively about the world. One might describe a tree, for example, by giving its type, its height, the color of its leaves and so on. The tree is an object to be described.

The oral storyteller, on the other hand, generally described the tree as a subject. They might speak of a tree as their friend, one in whom they find comfort, one who has provided solace for life.

Ninth, one of the purposes of the storyteller was to keep balance in the life of the people. Oral cultures live very much in the present which keeps itself in equilibrium by sloughing off memories and stories which no longer have present relevance. In his work on the Old Testament, Gerhard von Rad taught that each generation of Israel had to become Israel. They did this by bringing their story up to date. Some stories disappeared. New stories arose. Contrast the Deuteronomic History and the Chronicler's History, for example. Much of what these two histories tell covers the same historical period. The stories that are told, however, are very different because they were written in different generational settings. Each generation stitched stories together for its own time and place.

Finally, oral communities tell their stories in such a way that particular stories are the way to grasp more abstract or universal concepts. The particular is the way to the general. If one wished to describe the universal reality of fear one did not begin in the abstract by attempting to describe the dynamics of fear. One began with the particular. One told a story in which fear was a dominant motif.

This principle works just as well today. Good preaching should also begin with the particular as the way to the universal. As an old adage puts it: "one heart hit is universal."

I would like to engage in a bit of speculation. From these clues about communication in an oral-aural culture I would like to speculate on what form preaching might have taken in such a world. My thesis is that preaching is shaped by the communications culture of its time. How would oral-aural culture shape preaching?

1. Stitching Stories Together

First of all, preaching might have consisted in stitching stories together. This is really not speculation. We have the Old Testament as our witness. Old Testament stories, like the stories Homer knew, lived first in an oral environment. How, for example, did the book of Genesis come together? That is, of course, a highly complex question. At a simple level of the question, however, I think it is possible to maintain that those who put this material together had many stories to deal with and they asked themselves in what order they ought to stitch these stories together.

Much of the New Testament also shares in this story stitching modality. Think of the way Jesus communicated to us the reality of the Realm of God. He told stories. He said that the Realm of God is like a landowner who went out early in the morning to hire laborers for his vineyard. The Realm of God is as if someone would scatter seed on the ground. The Realm of God is like a mustard seed. The Realm of God is like a woman who took yeast and mixed it with three measures of flour.

Our systematic instincts, a gift from the world of print, urge us to organize Jesus' comments on the Realm of God in a more linear way. "The Realm of God has six characteristics . . . ."

The gospels are clear examples of stories being stitched together. We can see the gospel writers in our mind's eye with many, many stories at their disposal. Which stories are they to tell? In what order? Here, too, our linear instincts go to work. Instead of dwelling on the way Matthew or Mark or Luke stitched stories together we readily move to the more complex task of understanding the theology of Matthew. The relatively new biblical discipline of narrative criticism is a helpful tool in enabling us to discover the narrative or story character of much of biblical literature.

One of the things that struck me in my research in the world of oral-aural communication is the fact that stories that were stitched together did not have a linear plot line. At first I

23

was dumbstruck by this reality. My linear mind couldn't conceive of such a thing. A story has to be linear! It must move from a to z. It must move from beginning to ending. How else can one tell a story or many stories?

In an oral-aural culture stories were stitched together in an episodic manner. The goal of the story was not to move the listener along from point a to point z. The goal was that the listener participate in the inner life of the story: "The ancient listener or reader encountered the text not by having it 'explained' but by entering its world."[9] The goal of the storyteller is that the listener participates in the world of the story. This is one of the fundamental reasons that I believe that a return to the world of story in our preaching is so vital today. The gospel message told in story form invites people to participate in the very reality of its life.

One of the critiques that I have heard about the use of story in preaching is that the story category presents a problem because it is always a story out of the past. Preaching, the argument continues, is to be a present tense proclamation of God's saving grace. Because a story is out of the past it cannot be used for present tense proclamation. This criticism simply fails to understand the power of story to invite us into the reality of its world. We participate, in the present tense, when a powerful story is told.

Once I got over the initial shock and could see that stories could have a purpose other than developing a linear plot, I was able to find contemporary examples of this ancient art. I would maintain that most of the storytelling art of Garrison Keillor is precisely episodic and not linear in nature. When I listen to Keillor's stories on the radio or when I read them in his books I do not necessarily listen or read in order to move toward the resolution of the story. Keiller's stories very seldom resolve themselves. It is not because of the ending of the story that we listen and read so intently. We listen and read intently because we enjoy the journey itself. We go to Lake Wobegone in our imagination. We identify somehow with the populace of Lake Wobegone. We know these people! We are there. We participate. It is not the way the story ends that gives it its power over our imagination!

Keillor's stories highlight another characteristic of oral-aural culture. His stories are masterpieces of the way one moves from the particular to the universal. If I had been the program manager of a radio station 15 years ago and had been approached by Keillor to see if my station would carry his program, I'm sure I would have turned him away forthwith. Who in the world is interested in stories of Norwegians in a mythical town in Minnesota? As it turned out, people throughout the world are interested in Lake Wobegone. Keillor's stories are very particular stories of very particular people but they strike a universal chord in the human spirit. (Except perhaps with the people who actually live in rural Minnesota!) This living example of the universal relevance of a particular world is a very important fact to remember in regard to preaching! The particular is the best way to the universal!

2. The Use Of Repetition

The storyteller/preacher in the oral-aural world had to tell stories in such a way that the auditors could remember. This required the use of significant repetition. The auditors could not get printed copies or audio cassettes of the sermon. They took away what they heard and remembered. It was important, therefore, for the teller of the tale to tell it in such a way that it could be recalled by the listener.

Preaching in the African-American culture retains this strong use of repetition. We've all heard the advice of the African-American preacher who said he first tells people what he will tell them; then tells them; then tells them what he told them. African-American preaching is preaching that almost always has what I like to call a living center. There is a center, a focus to the presentation. That center is returned to again and again in the preaching event.

3. Situational Vs. Abstraction

Universal themes were treated through the instrumentality of particular stories. The tellers of the biblical stories had

25

wonderful stories to tell! It was through the telling of particular stories about Abraham and Moses and David and Jesus
that the preachers communicated the universal relevance of
God's self-revelation to Israel. The Jewish community has always been and remains basically a story-telling people of faith.
Our minds can follow people much better than they follow ideas. In my Lutheran tradition we have many complex
theological realities that we seek to communicate. Luther, for
example, believed that the Christian person was totally righteous and totally sinful at the same time *(simul justus et pecca-
tor)*. This is a very difficult reality to describe in the abstract.
It is not so difficult, however, to tell stories of people who
are saint and sinner simultaneously. I think of Peter in the
gospel story. In Matthew's story, chapter 16, we see Peter as
two different persons in almost the same moment. Peter answers Jesus' question about his identity. He says: "You are
the Messiah, the Son of the living God (Matthew 16:16)."

Jesus went on to tell the disciples that he must go to Jerusalem and undergo great suffering. Peter would have none of
it! "God forbid it, Lord! This must never happen to you."
And Jesus said: "Get behind me, Satan! You are a stumbling
block to me ... (Matthew 16:22)."

Peter. In one moment saint. In the very next moment sinner. We can recognize ourselves in such a story. We are much
like Peter. We are of two minds in relation to Jesus Christ.
We are saint and sinner in the same moment. A story that tells
a particular situation becomes for us the way to insight into
universal truth.

4. A Tone Of Conflict
Preaching joined the battle against the enemies of faith.
Preachers in a dominantly oral culture told the stories of the
Bible as a way of establishing their identity as the people of
God. It is the people of Israel, not the Canaanites, not the As-
syrians, not the Babylonians who are the people of God.
Storytelling/preaching served this end. Preaching established
Israel as the people of God. Preaching told stories of how God

did battle with chaos in order to bring this world and this people into existence. Preaching told stories of how God fights the battles of this people, Israel. Preaching told stories of how God brought this people out of bondage, through the sea, into a land flowing with milk and honey.

I indicated earlier that this tone of conflict was very much alive in Martin Luther. His preaching, too, had a strong tone of conflict. "He (Luther) preached as if the sermon were not a classroom, but a battleground! Every sermon was a battle for the souls of the people . . . a sermon was an apocalyptic event that set the doors of heaven and hell in motion, a part of the actual continuing conflict between the Lord and Satan."[10]

5. Right Brain Communication

Modern studies have established the difference between the work of our right brain and our left brain. The right hemisphere of the brain is, for example, holistic, artistic, symbolic, intuitive and creative. The left hemisphere of the brain is logical, mathematical, linear, sequential, intellectual and analytic.[11]

6. Metaphors Of Participation

Several years ago John Dominic Crossan made a distinction between two types of metaphors. Since story is really an extended metaphor it is useful to ask how the story form of metaphor works. Crossan distinguished between metaphors of illustration and metaphors of participation. ". . . there are metaphors in which information precedes participation so that the function of metaphor is to illustrate information about the metaphor's referent; but there are also metaphors in which participation precedes information so that the function of metaphor is to create participation in the metaphor's referent."[12]

To borrow the use of this understanding one would have to conclude that storytelling and preaching in the oral-aural culture told stories as metaphors of participation. The story was not an illustration of a point so that once one grasped the point the story was dispensable. These stories were rather metaphors of participation. The goal of the storyteller was to invite participation in the world of the story.

Contemporary literature in homiletics has picked up this distinction. In most contemporary works on homiletics the point is made that preaching must move from a time when stories were told as illustrations of intellectual points to a time when stories are told in such a way that the listener is grasped by the reality of the story through the story itself. The idea of using stories as illustrations for the ideas of a sermon has fallen on hard times.

7. Thinking In Story

The primary thinkers in early Israel were the storytellers. The hermeneutic of these early thinkers was a hermeneutic of "thinking in story." I am indebted to Thomas Boomershine for his pioneering work in this area. I still remember him making this point in a storytelling workshop which I attended. That was a powerful "Aha!" moment for me. Much of what I had been thinking about in terms of communication eras came together for me in that moment. Marshall McLuhan has also understood that myths, aphorisms and maxims, all forms of story, are characteristics of oral culture.

I hasten to add that "thinking in story" is an alternative way of thinking! It's not that "thinking in ideas" is real thinking and any other way of thinking is unthinkable. "Thinking in story" is certainly a mode of thinking that seems new to minds shaped by the linear massage of print. Thinking can be done in ideas; thinking can also be done in stories. "Thinking in story" is a gift given to us by oral-aural cultures which can be reappropriated today in a post-literate world.

8. Implications For Today's Preaching

It will be my argument in this work that the clues to the renewal of preaching to people in our communications culture lie in what I have projected to be the characteristics of preaching in oral-aural culture. Preaching, after all, is an oral form of communication! In my Lutheran tradition we speak much about the power of the word in baptism and the eucharist. We have not always understood as clearly that the preached word also has power. The spoken word reaches the interior of the listener. Sound, therefore, can be every bit as much a means of grace as water and bread and wine.

Preaching is oral communication. One of the great problems with preaching in our day is that preaching as we have come to know it is basically preaching formed under the conditions of literate culture. Literate preaching is in difficulty in a post-literate culture. Our modern world has been re-oralized by electronic communication. The world of silent print is behind us. Sound has returned to our ears through the communication media of radio and television. Walter Ong calls the world of electronic communication a "secondarily oral" world. Our present communication culture, based in electronic communication, has much in common with the oral-aural world of communication. I believe that one of the major sources for the renewal of preaching today will come through going back to the future. It is from a previous communication culture that we can find some of the guidance we need for preaching in our audio-visual world. The most important thing we can learn from our look "back to the future" is insight into an old/new way of thinking: thinking in story!

Preaching In A Literate Culture

Literate culture comes into being in two stages. The first stage is the development of writing and particularly the invention of the phonetic alphabet. The second stage of this era which encompasses most of Western human history is the invention of the printing press by Gutenberg in the 1450s. Stage one necessarily precedes stage two for without the phonetic alphabet there would have been no Gutenberg.

This movement from oral to literate culture represents a shift in the human sensorium. Oral-aural culture massaged the ear. A culture of writing massages the eye. As McLuhan often put it, Western civilization (we are not talking here about the world of the East) has given us an eye for an ear. It is this shift in sensory massage that we must comprehend in order to understand the enormous changes brought about through the invention of the alphabet.

Ivan Illich and Barry Sanders go so far as to say that it is alphabetic writing that brings the human race into existence. This is so because of the unique character of the phonetic alphabet which developed most fully in Greece somewhere around 720-700 B.C. "Pure, mature phonetic writing, which was discovered only once . . . is an oddity among writing systems in the same way that the loudspeaker is an oddity among trumpets. The alphabet records only sounds . . . . The alphabet does exactly the opposite of what most hieroglyphics and ideograms and, most importantly, what Semitic letters were created to do."[13]

It is important to notice this distinction made between Greek and Semitic culture. It is most probably the case that Hebrew culture, which did not use the phonetic alphabet, remained, perhaps precisely for this reason, an oral storytelling culture in contradistinction to the rational world of scientific thought developed by the Greeks. These differences in alphabet and sensory massage (eye or ear) produce enormous differences in the way in which theology has been done in the Western world. Early Christian theology soon left the world of the ear and entered the world of the eye. Is it not the case that the gospel writers were orally driven storytellers while Saint Paul was a literate Greek?

This matter of the uniqueness of the phonetic alphabet needs further comment. McLuhan puts it this way. "Only the phonetic alphabet makes a break between eye and ear, between semantic meaning and visual code; and thus only the phonetic writing has the power to translate man from the tribal to the civilized sphere, to give him an eye for an ear."[14] McLuhan asserts that no other people in the world have been able to develop a true alphabetic writing. "By the meaningless sign linked to the meaningless sound we have built the shape and meaning of Western man [sic]."[15] The Western world, that is, is a world of the eye. The ear is no longer necessary for learning. The western world is a world dominated by the sense of the eye.

Words on paper differ in many ways from words of speech. Words on paper take up space. They can be present all-at-once before our eyes as indeed the words on this page are all present for you simultaneously. Words can now be dissected into spatial parts. Words can be rearranged and recorded in many ways. The word processor, which is an extension of the eye, gives one a total sense of control of these words in space.

Those people who first worked with the phonetic alphabet experienced the beginning of a revolution! Their human consciousness was restructured by the linear massage of print![16] I would describe it as something like putting new "software" into the human brain. The mind learns how to think like an eye. The mind learns to think in linear patterns. As Ong puts it, "It appears no accident that formal logic was invented in an alphabetic culture."[17] McLuhan says, "The Greeks invented both their artistic and scientific novelties after the interiorization of the alphabet."[18] This new alphabetic software package for the brain changed the way humans think! ". . . during all our centuries of phonetic literacy we have favored the chain of inference as the mark of logic and reason."[19]

Humanity moved from ear to eye; from a world of hearing dominance to a world of sight dominance. This is also a movement, some suggest, from a culture dominated by right brain thought to a world dominated by left brain thought. Walter Ong quotes a scholar by the name of Kerckhove to this effect: ". . . more than other writing systems, the completely phonetic alphabet favors left-hemisphere activity in the brain, and thus on neurophysiological grounds fosters abstract, analytic thought."[20]

Print situates in space. Eugene Lowry, in his book titled, *Doing Time In The Pulpit*, indicates that this world of words on paper has come to dominate preaching in our time. Our current forms of preaching, that is, are forms shaped by the world of print; the world of the eye. He says that when he conducts preaching workshops he finds that almost every preacher he encounters, from whatever tradition, begins the sermon building task with the assumption that one must first structure one's ideas in space. I take this to mean that we all begin by formulating an outline which is a spatial way of putting our ideas together.

I mention Lowry at this point as a prelude of what is to come in terms of our preaching task today. Lowry wants to move us from structuring our sermons under the categories of space to ordering them under categories of time. He wants to move us, that is, from thinking in ideas to thinking in narrative event and experience. But we are getting ahead of our story.[21]

In the world of the eye, in the world of the linear massage, linearity now comes to dominate storytelling. Up until the time of print, Ong tells us, the only linearly plotted story line was that of the drama which from antiquity had been controlled by writing. We have spoken earlier of the fact that stories were told in an oral-aural culture in order for auditors to participate in the story and not necessarily to have them follow a linear plot.

The world of writing, that is, fundamentally changes the way thinking takes place. We must understand that this shift did not come about instantly with the development of the phonetic alphabet. Very few people in any culture were educated in the ways of writing and reading. For perhaps as many as 2,000 years the world of orality and the world of writing lived side by side. The educated elite lived in the world of writing. They are the ones who have passed the culture on to us. The culture as we have received it, therefore, is a culture of ideas and abstract thought. The world of the ordinary citizen remained very much an oral world. It is only in the late middle ages that writing begins to take hold of the whole culture. Even then vestages of oral culture were powerful. Those who could read, for example, usually read aloud. Sound was still a part of the culture. Saint Augustine, for example, was stunned that Ambrose could read without making any sounds! The world of silent print had not as yet developed.

It is in stage two of the communications culture of writing that the impress of linearity begins to shape whole cultures. This transition comes with the development of the printing press in the 1450s. The printing press democratized the linear eye massage and set the stage for a rapid shift in human consciousness. Walter Ong puts it this way, "Thus the development of writing and print ultimately fostered the breakup of feudal societies and the rise of individualism. Writing and print created the isolated thinker, the man with the book, and downgraded the network of personal loyalties which oral cultures favor as matrices of communication . . . "[22]

McLuhan says: ". . . print carries the individuating power of the phonetic alphabet much further than manuscript culture could ever do. Print is the technology of individualism."[23]

Descartes signified this shift into an individuated culture when he said, "I think, therefore I am." An individual thinker, cut off from human community, could now make a unique claim to individual being. That's only possible when one is surrounded by books, by the world of silent print, as companions in thought. Humans in an oral culture might have said something like: "We talk, therefore, we are."

We recognize immediately that Martin Luther is a modern man, a man of print. Against the weight of empire and church, against the weight of accepted human communities, Luther could say: "Here I stand." And there he stood, with his books. So it was in the church. Authority in the medieval church was vested in the teaching office of the church. Authority was vested in people. Luther stood with the book of the Bible and his own books against this traditional world.[24]

The very locus of believing changed. With the advent of the world of print we come to a world where seeing is believing. That is a far remove from the oral world where hearing is believing.

I did not realize until I moved into the world of media how far reaching is the significance of the printing press for

Protestant tradition. Much of Luther's success as a reformer can be attributed to the fact that the printing press was at hand and his material could be spread far and wide. No reformer prior to Luther had this technology available. The interesting thing to me is that Luther appears to remain a quite oral person in the midst of this emerging literate world. Much of the material that we have from Luther comes from the notes of his students. Luther delivered the material orally and it was brought to print later.

I believe that it is true to say of the Lutheran Church that it is the first church in the history of the world to be helped to birth and helped to definition by the mass media. That mass media, of course, is print. Luther, therefore, who is very much an oral person, becomes probably the first mass media figure in human history. Some authorities say that Luther's German Bible was the first mass media product that had an impact on the daily life of people. His Bible translation gave the German people a common language.

Pierre Babin quotes Richard Molard to the following effect: "Protestantism was born with printing and has been the religion in which printing — the printed Bible, the catechism, newspapers, and journals — has played a vital part. The present crisis in these publications is undoubtedly a sign of a very deep crisis of identity. How is it possible to be a Protestant in a world in which radio and television are the easiest forms of communication?"[25]

Molard begins to point to the crisis now faced by literate protestantism. For the moment, however, let us reflect a bit further on the very deep connection between protestantism and print. Something as simple as Luther's *Catechism* became a bestseller. Here was a whole new way of teaching! And it was standardized. Uniform. Everyone had the same information. Lutherans, a people of the book, would later craft the *Augsburg Confession* and gather all their basic documents in a book: *The Book of Concord,*1580. Lutheranism and books belong together. It was not possible until the invention of the printing press to make use of books in this way. Prior to the standardized possibilities brought by print authority had to rest in the hands of people!

Zwingli and Calvin moved even further into the print ordered world. In the arena of worship, for example, Luther basically kept the liturgy which the church had handed down and purged it of the elements that he thought were doctrinally suspect. Zwingli and Calvin used a book, the Bible, as the ordering power of worship life. "The radical reshaping of the liturgy by Zwingli denied any such sacramental relationship; materiality and faith were separated. The believer was oriented to God solely by faith and scripture. Christian worship centered not on the eucharist but on the reading, hearing and interpretation of the Bible. Emptied of visual images, liturgical space became a place in which preaching and the reading of scripture were paramount."[26]

The mainline Protestant churches are churches largely shaped by the technology of print. That is a very large part of the dilemma facing these churches today. Print technology is being replaced by electronic technology. Churches that were born out of their ability to function with the new technology of print must now make an adjustment to the world of electronic communication. The success of these churches into the 21st century will depend a great deal upon their ability to adapt to today's media.

Print media, of course, did not conquer the world in a day. It took time for print to become established as the communications media of the day. Most sources indicate that it was not until the 18th century that print media became dominant in the western world. According to Neil Postman, 18th and 19th century America may have been the most dominant print culture that had existed up until that time. Gregor Goethals suggests that the strength of Christianity in America, shaped by the tradition of Calvin and Zwingli, is at least partly responsible for this fact.[27] Postman indicates that the literacy rates in early American life were very high. Books sold at astounding rates. The book most widely read was the Bible.

35

Postman, in his book titled, *Amusing Ourselves to Death: Public Discourse in the Age of Show Business*, is fascinated by literate America. His book is a lament about the loss of print-shaped America. He cites Aldous Huxley's *Brave New World* approvingly. Huxley predicted that we would fall in love with our new technologies and become enslaved to them. George Orwell, in *1984*, was wrong. Our new technology did not become Big Brother watching over us with a menacing glance. As Postman puts it: "Big Brother turns out to be Howdy Doody."[28] In other words, we are being enslaved by our new technologies but we don't recognize our slavery. In fact, we like what we see and hear. We are, as his book title puts it, amusing ourselves to death.

Postman's work is very much relevant to a book on preaching. As you will have noticed, the subtitle of his book indicates that he is really interested in the shape of public discourse. Peaching, of course, is public discourse. Preaching is not the subject of Postman's book but his comments are very helpful in understanding how public discourse has been changed in America. Here is the thesis of his work. ". . . this book is an inquiry into and a lamentation about the most significant American cultural fact of the second half of the 20th century: the decline of the Age of Typography and the ascendancy of the Age of Television. This change-over has dramatically and irreversibly shifted the content and meaning of public discourse, since two media so vastly different cannot accommodate the same ideas."[29]

My overall thesis is basically similar to Postman's. Electronic technology is taking over from print technology. Discourse is changing. I am more optimistic than Postman that the public discourse of preaching can adapt itself to this new technology. Before we come to that discussion, however, we need to note Postman's very important contribution as he discusses how discourse is shaped by typography. Postman is very helpful in understanding what literate discourse is all about.

"In the 18th and 19th centuries, religious thought and institutions in America were dominated by an austere, learned

36

and intellectual form of discourse that is largely absent from religious life today."[30] The point that he is making is very important. He shows us how print shapes oratory! The lineal, analytical structure of print was mirrored in the expository prose of the day. He draws three conclusions for the shape of discourse when the Typographic Mind is at work.

1. Oratory, including preaching, that is based on the written word has a propositional content. It communicates ideas. In a print culture one learns to think in ideas. (Remember that in an oral culture one learned to think in stories.) "Whenever language is the principal of communication — especially language controlled by the rigors of print — an idea, a fact, a claim is the inevitable result . . . there is no escape from meaning when language is the instrument guiding one's thought."[31]

2. Oratory based on print is serious discourse because it demands to be understood. ". . . when an author and reader are struggling with semantic meaning, they are engaged in the most serious challenge to the intellect."[32]

3. Oratory based on print follows a line of thought. It is crafted as a rational argument. "In a culture dominated by print, public discourse tends to be characterized by a coherent, orderly arrangement of facts and ideas . . . . It is not by accident that the Age of Reason was coexistent with the growth of print culture."[33]

Postman reflects also upon the preaching of the time. He tells us that the great preachers of the age were highly literate in their presentation. Jonathan Edwards, he writes, ". . . read his sermons, which were tightly knit and closely reasoned expositions of theological doctrine. Audiences may have been moved emotionally by Edward's language, but they were, first and foremost, required to understand it."[34]

Postman, therefore, would posit that preaching based on the Typographic Mind (his term) would be a communication of ideas following a line of thought toward the goal that people could understand what was being communicated. As I gave Postman's theses some thought I realized that this was exactly how I was taught to preach. Preaching was about the proper ordering of ideas. I didn't take any advanced courses in preaching when I was in seminary. The basic advanced course that was offered was a study of the great literate preachers of the 19th century. I doubt that anyone would offer such an advanced course in preaching today. The literate preaching of the 19th century would simply not work in our post-literate world.

Thomas Troeger, in his work titled *Imagining A Sermon,* gives a summary of what literate preaching is like that echoes much of what Postman has just said. Troeger tells us that when the classical rhetoric of Greece dominated what he calls "the city of homiletical wisdom," that city gave instruction that preaching should be:

- the clarity of the argument;
- the logic of the outline;
- the tightness of the transitions;
- the development of the main point;
- the persuasiveness of the reasoning;
- how well the illustrations fit the principles;
- and the theological defensibility of the message.[35]

The dominant motif of Postman's book is his establishment of the fact that public discourse has been so radically altered by the advent of electronic media that the kind of serious, propositional, linear discourse of the past will not work anymore. He cites the Lincoln-Douglas debates as an example. They debated the issues for seven hours a day and did not feel they had time to fully explore the issues. In our day we get presidential debates that call for a two minute answer, a two minute response and a one minute rebuttal! Television has given us a peek-a-boo world of rapid fire information coming at us in small bits and pieces. Sound bytes on the evening news have shrunk from 45 seconds a few years back to 10 to 15 today. Postman argues, and it is difficult to disagree, that television is changing public discourse. It has become difficult, if not impossible, to communicate serious ideas through this medium! I think Postman is essentially correct in his analysis.

In a chapter titled "Shuffle Off to Bethlehem," Postman applies his thesis to religion and television. He believes that television is equally inimical to the presentation of serious religious ideas. In the first place, television is presented without apology as entertainment. "Everything that makes religion an historic, profound and sacred human activity is stripped away; there is no ritual, no dogma, no tradition, no theology, and above all no sense of spiritual transcendence."[36]

Secondly, he argues that television preachers cannot begin to compare to the great learning, theological subtlety and powerful expositional skills of the great literate preachers. "What makes these television preachers the enemy of religious experience is not so much their weakness but the weaknesses of the medium in which they work ... not all forms of discourse can be converted from one medium to another."[37]

Postman makes a powerful case that television has changed the nature of public discourse. I agree with his argument. It is certainly true that the political environment has suffered because of the peek-a-boo style in which political ideas are now presented. Images count more than substance. This is a real problem.

I do not, however, agree with Postman when he applies his argument to religion and television. Postman believes that "literate" Christianity is doomed by electronic forms of communication. We will no longer be able to communicate our faith in the literate manner to which most of us have been accustomed. Postman's problem is that he equates the content of Christianity with the massage of the eye, with the form of thought created by print. What must be remembered is that the world of the Bible has been handed on from generation to generation for hundreds of years prior to the development of the printing press. The Christian faith does not need literate culture in order to communicate its message! And how did they do it? They told stories! If we told stories in the past as a way of thinking, as a way of communicating our faith, we can do it again today. We can go "back to the future" to find a way to communicate the biblical story in a post-literate world. That will be the burden of my next chapter. We can learn again how to "think in stories."

Characteristics Of Print-shaped Preaching

I would like to close this chapter by listing what seem to me to be the basic characteristics of preaching under the impress of print. It ought to be clear that print-shaped preaching has taken many patterns over the ages. It does seem to me, however, that one can extrapolate from the history of preaching certain common characteristics. Having read a goodly number of homiletics textbooks, and having given a good deal of thought to the nature of preaching in a print-driven world, I would propose the following characteristics:

1. Sermons are linear in nature.

We joke a lot in the world of homiletics about sermons that are "three points and a poem." It is assumed in the Lutheran tradition that the three point sermon is a "Lutheran" sermon. Not so! Three point sermons have been around for an incredibly long time. In 1322 Robert of Basevorn wrote an influential treatise on preaching titled, *The Form of Preaching*. Basevorn, as others in his day, prescribes a sermon in six parts: (1) theme: a scriptural quotation; (2) protheme: introduction of the theme followed by a prayer; (3) repetition of theme with explanation of the sermon's purpose; (4) division or partition of theme (usually into threes) with 'authorities' of various sorts to 'prove' each division; (5) subdivision of theme; (6) amplification of each division."[38]

Basevorn makes this argument for three points: ". . . in this method of preaching only three statements, or the equivalent of three, are used in the theme — either from respect to the Trinity, or because of a threefold cord is not easily broken, or because this method is most followed by Bernard, or, as I think more likely, because it is more convenient for the set time of the sermon."[39]

Or consider Francois Fenelon (1651-1715) who wrote the first modern (in the world of print) rhetoric. He tells us that in every sermon there ought to be an orderly succession of proofs. He summarizes this way: "First, principles; then facts;

and from these draw the conclusions which you desire to reach; taking care to arrange the reasoning in such a manner as that the proofs will admit of being borne in mind easily ... the hearer should feel more and more the growing weight of truth.''[40]

Literate preaching is linear preaching!

2. *Structures ideas in space.*

I believe Lowry is correct when he informs us that the first task preachers do under the canons of print in preparing a sermon is to "structure their ideas in space." First, we get an outline on paper. With that done we are well on the way.

3. *Sermons contain propositions as the main points.*

Preaching under the impress of literate culture is fundamentally about the delivery of ideas. The classic rhetorical tradition of Greece came to dominate the form of Christian preaching early on. Saint Augustine endorsed this tradition and his work on preaching dominated Christian thought about preaching for many centuries. Greek rhetoric placed a heavy emphasis on the logic of persuasion. Ideas reigned!

Alan of Lille, the author of the first systematic treatment of homiletics in the 800 years since Saint Augustine, argued clearly that preaching is about forming hearers through the path of reason. "Preaching is an open and public instruction in faith and behavior, whose purpose is the forming of men (sic); it derives from the path of reason.''[41]

4. *Sermons are analytical in nature.*

The task of preaching is to analyze the ideas of a text. Texts that are narrative in nature are analyzed to find their ideas! The sermon is then formulated around the ideas. The narrative is left behind!

5. *Left-brain communication.*

Those things which characterize the activity of the left hemisphere of the brain dominate the preaching task.

6. Metaphors of illustration.

Stories are used to illustrate the points of the sermon. They are dispensable once the listener has the point.

In his book, *The Cry For Myth,* Rollo May asserts that there are two main ways in which human beings have communicated. One is a rationalistic language. "This is specific and empirical, and eventuates in logic. In this kind of communication the persons who are speaking the words are irrelevant to the truth or falsehood of what they say."[42]

The second way in which humans communicate, May claims, is by way of myth. May defines myth as ". . . a drama which begins as a historical event and takes on its special character as a way of orienting people to reality. The myth, or story, carries the values of the society . . . . The narration always points toward totality rather than specificity; it is chiefly a right brain function . . . . Whereas empirical language refers to objective facts, myth refers to the quintessence of human experience, the meaning and significance of human life. The whole person speaks to us, not just the brain.[43]

May's analysis is an excellent summary of two ways of human communication; two ways in which the brain functions to communicate reality to others. In literate culture it has basically been the case that preaching has communicated through "rationalistic language." Preaching has been a left brain operation. Earlier human cultures communicated the meaning of reality by telling stories. Preaching in such cultures was more of a right brain operation. Preaching in our time will need to make use of both ways of human communicating. Human communication in our time has until very recently been dominated by the left brain. We will need to learn some lessons from oral cultures in order to learn to think also in more wholistic, right brain patterns.

7. Thinking in ideas.

It is pretty much assumed in this world of thought that the task of preaching is the presentation of ideas. This is how one thinks. We study texts in search of ideas. Once we have our ideas the sermon comes into shape. Commentaries are a great help in this matter and they, too, are chiefly about the ideas found in the text. The hermeneutical premise is that thinking in ideas is the way to discover and present the material.

In the chart below the characteristics of preaching shaped in an oral culture are placed side by side with the characteristics of preaching shaped by a literate culture.

Preaching In An Oral Culture	Preaching In A Literate Culture
1. Stitching stories together.	Linear development of ideas.
2. Use of repetition.	Structure ideas in space.
3. Situational vs. abstraction.	Propositions as the main points.
4. A tone of conflict.	Analytical in nature.
5. Right brain communication.	Left brain communication.
6. Metaphors of participation.	Metaphors of illustration.
7. Thinking in story.	Thinking in ideas.

---

1. Walter Ong, *The Presence of the Word*, (Minneapolis, University of Minnesota Press, 1967) p. 17.
2. See the discussion in Ong., *Ibid.,* pp. 111-138.
3. Ivan Illich and Barry Sanders, *The Alphabetization of the Popular Mind,* (New York, Vintage Books, 1989) pp. 15, 18, 19.
4. *Ibid.,* p. 24.
5. Walter Ong, *Orality and Literacy: The Technologizing of the Word,* (New York, Methuen, 1982) p. 28.
6. *Ibid.,* Chapter 3, pp. 31-49.
7. Marshall McLuhan, *The Gutenberg Galaxy: The Making of Typographic Man,* (Toronto, The University of Toronto Press, 1962) p. 27.
8. Richard A. Jensen, *Telling The Story: Variety and Imagination in Preaching,* (Minneapolis, Augsburg, 1980) p. 38.
9. Don M. Wardlaw, editor, *Preaching Biblically: Creating Sermons in the Shape of Scripture,* (Philadelphia, Westminster Press, 1983) p. 34.
10. Fred W. Meuser, *Luther The Preacher,* (Minneapolis, Augsburg, 1983) p. 25.
11. See Pierre Babin, *The New Era in Religious Communication,* (Minneapolis, Fortress Press, 1991) p. 55 for a complete chart of left hemisphere and right hemisphere functions of the brain.
12. John Dominic Crossan, *In Parables: The Challenge of the Historical Jesus,* (New York, Harper & Row, 1973) p. 14.

13. Ivan Illich, *op. cit.,* p. 9.
14. McLuhan, *Gutenberg, op cit.,* p. 38.
15. *Ibid.,* p. 65.
16. See Ong, *Orality, op. cit.,* Chapter 4 titled: "Writing restructures consciousness."
17. Ong, *Presence, op. cit.,* p. 45.
18. McLuhan, *op. cit.,* p. 75.
19. McLuhan, *Understanding, op. cit.,* p. 87.
20. Ong, *Orality, op. cit.,* p. 91.
21. Eugene L. Lowry, *Doing Time in the Pulpit: The Relationship Between Narrative and Preaching,* (Nashville, Abingdon Press, 1985).
22. Ong, *Presence, op. cit.,* p. 54.
23. McLuhan, *Gutenberg, op. cit.,* p. 193.
24. "The new homogeneity of the printed page seemed to inspire a subliminal faith in the validity of the printed Bible as bypassing the traditional oral authority of the church, on one hand, and the need for rational critical scholarship on the other. It was as if print, uniform and repeatable commodity that it was, had the power of creating a new hypnotic superstition of the book as independent of and uncontaminated by human agency. Nobody who had read manuscripts could achieve this state of mind concerning the nature of the written word." *Ibid.,* p. 176.
25. Pierre Babin, *The New Era in Religious Communication,* (Minneapolis, Fortress Press, 1991) p. 25.
26. Gregor T. Goethals, *The Electronic Golden Calf: Images, Religion and the Making of Meaning,* (Cambridge, Cowley Publications, 1990) p. 50.
27. *Ibid.,* p. 55.
28. Neil Postman, *Amusing Ourselves to Death: Public Discourse in the Age of Show Business,* (New York, Penguin Books, 1985) p. 111.
29. *Ibid.,* p. 8.
30. *Ibid.,* p. 55.
31. *Ibid.,* p. 50.
32. *Ibid.*
33. *Ibid.,* p. 51.
34. *Ibid.,* p. 54.
35. Thomas Troeger, *Imagining A Sermon* (Nashville, Abingdon Press, 1990) p. 29.
36. Postman, *op. cit.,* pp. 116-117.
37. *Ibid.,* p. 117.
38. Richard Lischer, *Theories of Preaching: Selected Readings in the Homiletical Tradition,* (Durham, The Labyrinth Press, 1987) p. 219.
39. *Ibid.,* p. 220.
40. *Ibid.,* p. 229.
41. *Ibid.,* p. 10.
42. Rollo May, *The Cry For Myth*, (New York, Bantam Doubleday Dell Publishing Group, Inc., 1991) p. 26.
43. *Ibid.*

CHAPTER TWO
Preaching In
A Post-literate Age

1. The Post-literate World
In terms of human communication we are living through a time of cataclysmic change. On the one hand, things are always changing. One certainly comes to understand and appreciate that the longer one lives. "All is change." But the change to a new communications environment is change of a different order. We are living through only the second communications change in the history of humankind. Humankind moved from oral-aural culture to a culture first of writing and then of print. This change took thousands of years. Today, it is changing again. We are moving from the world of print into an age of electronic communication.

Marshall McLuhan puts it this way:

"An age in rapid transition is one which exists on the frontier between two cultures and between conflicting technologies. Every moment of its consciousness is an act of translation of each of these cultures into the other. Today we live on the frontier between five centuries of mechanism and the new electronics, between the homogeneous and the simultaneous. The 16th century Renaissance was an age on the frontier between 2,000 years of alphabetic and manuscript culture, on the one hand, and the new mechanism of repeatability and quantification, on the other."[1]

This change has enormous consequences for the Christian church. Unfortunately, the church hardly seems to be aware of the enormity of the change that is at hand. We speak today of the crisis of mainline (some call them the "sideline") churches in America. I believe that the root of the crisis in the church is its failure to recognize and adapt to the quickly dawning world of electronic communications. People are being changed by their media. In order to speak to changed people the church must speak in changed ways. This kind of change, however, comes very slowly to the church.

There is a significant segment of the Christian church that is quite successful in speaking to the changed people of this electronic environment. Those churches whose roots until recently were steeped in oral culture have made the adaptation to the "secondarily oral" world of electronic quite successfully. The churches that have been effective in their use of television, for example, are by and large the churches with oral roots. The Pentecostals lead the parade! Just about every single successful Christian television program that has had success with the public has been of Pentecostal origin. These made-for-TV preachers learned their trade on the "sawdust trail." They are superb oral communicators. What they do best works on television. This lies in marked contrast to the failure of the "literate" churches to master the new media.

In this work my concern is with preaching. As the media changes, and as people are changed by the media, preaching must undergo significant change in order to communicate effectively. The literate preaching styles of the last several centuries must be expanded. Something new is called for by the communications media of our time. Many contemporary works on homiletics sense this need for change and propose helpful new paths. I have learned much from my colleagues. What I miss in their works, however, is an overarching framework for the need for change in our time. I am convinced that it is the shift from a literate to a post-literate communications culture that calls forth changes in the way we conceptualize the preaching task in our time. I hope that this work will be at least an initial step in providing a framework for thinking about the task of preaching in a world of changing communications environment.

Tony Schwarz, a student of McLuhan, gives the following helpful definition of what is meant by a post-literate age. "We have become a post-literate society. Electronic media rather than the printed word are now our major means of non-face-to-face communication."[2]

In other words, face-to-face communication is always the dominant means of communication in any culture. Until very recently, if we were not getting information from people in face-to-face encounter, we were getting that information from the printed word. Today that ratio has changed. Radio and television have replaced print as the second most common way in which we receive information.

Schwarz indicates that it is only in a time of media change that we notice our media at all. Reading, for example, has been a major means of communication for centuries. While we were busily engaged in reading we didn't stop and think how the very act of reading changed and shaped us. "The structure of print communication became the structure of a 'logical mind' in our society. Because print was the dominant means of communication for so long, we lost sight of its role as a medium and its effect upon thought and knowledge. Therefore, we were not prepared for the challenge that would occur when a new communication medium appeared."[3]

This is precisely the point I want to make about preaching. We have been preaching three-point, linear, logical, analytical sermons for a long time! What we have often failed to do, however, is to understand that this form of preaching was given its shape by the form of the human communication of writing and print. As we move from a literate to a post-literate era we must become cognizant of the impact of media on our preaching and ask how preaching in our time might be shaped by our electronic forms of communication.

The massage of today's media is a new massage. Oral-aural communication massaged the ear. Writing and print communication massaged the eye. Electronic communication and particularly television, stimulates and massages many of our senses simultaneously. We live in an age of the polymorphic massages of our senses. As we shall see the effect of this polymorphic massage is a more complete participation of our sensate selves in the new media. Participation, physical/sensate participation, is one of the hallmarks of the new age.

How shall we date the dawn of the era of electronic communication? McLuhan suggests the importance of Einstein's discovery of curved space. "With this recognition of curved space in 1905 the Gutenberg Galaxy was officially dissolved. With the end of lineal specialisms and fixed points of view, compartmentalized knowledge became as unacceptable as it has always been irrelevant."[4] He goes on to say that it was with the invention of the telegraph in 1837 that the first invasion was made into the fixed world of print. The inventions of note that have propelled this era forward are the telegraph, the telephone, the phonograph, the photograph, the electric light, radio, movies and television. I have sometimes facetiously suggested that the electronic age will have dawned in its fullest when there is a computer in every classroom and a VCR in every living room. That day is rapidly approaching!

Most students of this communication shift see the invention of television and television's subsequent domination of human life as the quantum leap into a new era. Television is a dominant medium! It is estimated that most people spend 80 percent of their non-working and non-sleeping time watching television. Data that we have gathered in the Evangelical Lutheran Church in America supports this assertion with the significant exception of the clergy. The lives of lay people are much more plugged into an electronic environment than are the lives of clergy. Laypeople and clergy experience a different massage! This may cause a communications gap between clergy and lay people. If this communications gap is not bridged preaching may not hit its mark!

The role of clergy in the world of communication is an important role to note. It was not long ago, in a solidly literate culture, that the pastor was one of the most literate persons in town. This highly literate status of the clergy commanded a good deal of prestige. But times have changed. Clergy as a class of people are by no means the most skilled persons in a world of electronic communication. Our children are often our teachers in the ways of electronic media. If it weren't for my youngest son and my son-in-law I wouldn't know how to manage most of my new electronic gadgets. It may be that this change in the proficiency status of the clergy from one media culture to another affects clergy prestige in our culture as well.

1985 is a year of significance in the shift of communications cultures. 1985 was the first year that more videocassettes were checked out/rented from video stores than there were books checked out of libraries. Many libraries, of course, have now become videobraries as well. The videocassettes that we checked out were playing on our VCR. The VCR was a very significant invention in heightening the pace of the electronic massage. I have been told that the VCR saturated the marketplace faster than any other big ticket manufactured item.

The advent of electronic means of communication does not mean that people no longer read. More books are published in our time than ever before. Questions have been raised, however, as to whether people actually read the books they buy. A New York woman told me that it was the fashion in one of the book clubs that she was aware of in New York City that people only read the reviews. They meet to discuss the reviews! Few persons actually read the books. I've heard similar examples from elsewhere. At any rate, the coming of a new communications age does not replace the age that preceded it. People still read. What has changed, however, is the total massage of the human sensorium. We are massaged more often and more deeply by electronic communication today than we ever were by print communication.

Walter Ong tells us that in the past century the word has entered a new stage beyond orality, script and print. This is a stage characterized by the use of electronics. Ong notes that this stage of communication is a return to orality. Sound returns to the world of words. Sound, of course, was the major characteristic of words in an oral-aural world. Under the aegis of print, words gradually lost their sound. The world of "silent print" came into being. Radio and television put the sound back into words. This is one of the reasons some people speak of the emerging electronic culture as "secondarily oral." The new culture has sound in its words as did the oral-aural era that preceded it by many centuries.

"As the word moves from sound into space and then re-structures itself electronically into sound in a new way, the sensorium is recognized and man's (sic) relationship to the physical world around him, to his fellow men, to his own thought, and to himself radically changes."[5]

I've suggested that this is a time of cataclysmic change. Ong suggests that it is, indeed, the end of the modern age. "The modern age was thus much more the child of typography than it has commonly been made out to be . . . largely by reason of this fact, the modern age is now a thing of the past."[6] The world of the enlightenment is basically co-terminus with the world of print and print's massage of the human consciousness.

McLuhan has suggested that post-modern humans live in a new global village. This global village comes into being through the speed of electronic communication. The events in Europe in 1989, for example, are a primary example of this global village. The countries in eastern Europe cast off their past like dominoes. We watched it in our homes! So did the people in Europe. Each new revolution was a copy of the last one. People in one nation watched on television as a sister nation staged her revolution in the streets. The next day they were on the streets.

Marshall McLuhan is famous for his division of media into hot media and cool media. Let's review his definition. "A hot medium is one that extends one single sense in 'high definition.' High definition is the stage of being well filled with data . . . . Telephone is a cool medium, or one of low definition, because the ear is given a meager amount of information. And speech is a cool medium of low definition, because so little is given and so much has to be filled in by the listener . . . hot media do not leave so much to be filled in or completed by the audience. Hot media are, therefore, low in participation, and cool media are high in participation."[7]

In the literate culture that has preceded us, according to McLuhan, manuscripts were cool; print was hot. Print had been our dominant media. Print provided us with all the information we needed to grasp its meaning. Print was high in data, low in participation. We participated only with our eyes. Participation, in McLuhan's lexicon, is a physical reality. He is talking about the physical participation of our sensory organs. This understanding of participation must be kept clearly in view. McLuhan describes the dominant communication means of our time, television, as a cool medium. The move from print to television is a move from hot to cool. The move from print to television is a move from a media that demands little physical/sensate participation to a media that demands much physical/sensate participation.

McLuhan is often misunderstood on this point. Inevitably people complain when I explain his thesis that television calls for greater participation than print. They say that they participate just as much, maybe more, in reading a novel than they do when they watch a story on television. That is not the kind of participation McLuhan is talking about. For McLuhan participation is about the physical engagement of our senses. We use more of our senses in watching television than we do in reading a book. Many books can lay open on a coffee table in the center of a room. Their presence does not engage our senses. But turn the television set on. When the television set is turned on our senses are immediately stimulated. It is very difficult to keep one's eyes off a television set if it is playing in the room. We are physically drawn in to its world.

To fully understand this change we need to have some kind of understanding of how television works. McLuhan again: "The mode of the television image has nothing in common with film or photo, except that it offers also a non-verbal *gestalt* or posture of forms. With television, the viewer is the screen. He is bombarded with light impulses .... The television image is visually low in data. The television image is not a still shot. It is not a photo in any sense but a ceaselessly forming contour of things limned by the scanning-finger .... The television image offers three million dots per second to the

51

receiver. From these he accepts only a few dozen each instant, from which to make an image .... the viewer of the television mosaic, with technical control of the image, unconsciously reconfigures the dots into an abstract work of art .... The television image requires each instant that we 'close' the spaces in the mesh by a convulsive sensuous participation that is profoundly kinetic and tactile ...."[8]

In other words, watching television is hard work! Our senses are working very hard whether we realize it or not. This is participation! Pierre Babin describes this physical participation in the new audio-visual media as modulation. "I believe that modulation is the essence of audiovisual language, as words and their sequence are the essence of written language. The term modulation is deliberately used here because of its physical and technical meanings. Practically speaking, modulation indicates vibration frequencies, which vary in length, intensity, harmonics and other nuances. These vibrations are perceived by our senses and induce emotions, images, even ideas ...!"[9]

To understand modulation and this physical participation in electronic media one has only to watch a teenager walking down the street with his or her Walkman turned on. This young person is wired into sound. That's how I understand Babin. The new media work us over physically as if we were wired into them. It's as if our body is plugged into these media and physically receives input. Our sensorium is deeply involved. We are physically engaged. Our whole being is massaged. This is a very different world than the "hot" world of the book and the eye! Preaching to people accustomed to this cool massage is the new challenge. Ideas for their minds to mull will probably not engage them sufficiently in the preaching process.

Understanding the power of television to attract our attention requires also a grasp of the incredibly fast pace at which things move on television. Commercials change edits, scenes, on the average of every two seconds! Every two seconds we are looking at a different scene. That pace is even faster on MTV. The programs themselves move quickly. On the basic evening television story we see only a couple of minutes at a time of a particular story line. Then we shift to another story and another and back to the first and so on. Soap operas also work this way. We are processing several stories at once. This, too, demands participation!

It should not be difficult to understand why people who watch television during 80 percent of their non-working, non-sleeping hours find the pace of the average worship service boring. They are not bored with Jesus. They are bored with the hot service they are attending. People weaned on the cool medium of television have great difficulty with the hot effect of most worship services. I have sometimes said of my church that it is a hot church in a cool world. There is a great challenge before us.

Rev. Derek Weber recently did research at the University of Edinburgh in media and theological education. His unpublished work is titled: *Preaching To Be Heard in A Television Age.* He makes some remarkably good points on the way to understand how the church can begin to meet the challenge of the post-literate age.

Weber notes that television has brought about a new language and method of communication. The language of the book, he tells us, is guided by rationality, deductive organization and logic. But the book has given way to television which speaks the language of image and suggestion. Television language, he says, is a language of narrative and emotion. Preaching, he concludes, must adopt a new kind of language and be presented with an awareness of the visual communication of body and face. Ideas, he writes, must give way to images. Understanding must give way to experience. Drama will work because it massages both eye and ear. Preachers need to see themselves as dramatists.

In his work Weber cites a book titled, *Mind and Media,* by Patricia Marks Greenfield. Ms. Greenfield indicates that studies have proven that children are capable of parallel processing. In parallel processing a person is able to take in and assimilate multiple pieces of information simultaneously.

The older pattern for assimilating information was serial processing, processing information one piece at a time. This means that children really can listen to their music and do their homework at the same time. They have learned to do two things at once! Needless to say, many of these children will be bored by the normally paced worship service and sermon! When we think of worship and preaching for the future we must take this possibility of parallel processing very seriously or risk losing those who are capable of assimilating multiple pieces of information at the same time.

Weber strongly believes that the perceptive apparatus of people in our pews has been changed by electronic media. Because the hearers have changed, preaching must change. I agree with Weber. It seems to me that there are only two alternatives to the need for a change in our preaching. We can assume that the electronic culture does not affect people fundamentally so that change is not needed. Or, and I have seen this case made publicly, we can decry the change as inimical to the way we need to communicate the Christian message and work to change people back to the way they were in the world of print so that we can communicate with them the way we always have. The thesis of my work is that our form of preaching must change in order to speak to post-literate humanity.

The change that must take place is argued very effectively by Walter Wangerin, a Lutheran pastor and writer, in a *Resource* cassette produced by Augsburg Publishing House in 1989. Wangerin asserts that there are two fundamental modes of communication. He calls these two modes the explanatory and the evocative/invocative. I think one could use the label "literate" for the explanatory mode and "oral" for the evocative/invocative mode. In the explanatory mode, Wangerin asserts, one seeks to explain ideas so that the hearer understands. Wangerin claims that in this mode of communication the burden of doing is upon the hearer. The hearer is the doer. He/she must do something with the ideas presented. The hearer is the doer; the ideas are the "done to."

54

It seems to me that this explanatory mode as a medium of communication for the gospel is very problematic. Let us say we are preaching a sermon whose basic proposition is that God justifies sinners by grace through faith alone. In the explanatory mode the living reality of justification is reduced to an idea. The hearer succeeds when he/she understands the idea. In this kind of presentation faith is always defined as believing the right ideas. The hearer must understand and believe. That's the law of how this form of communication works. This mode of communication changes the gospel from the power of God which takes hold of one's life into an idea which the hearer must understand. No matter how much one talks about grace in this schema the hearer is "saved" by the good work of understanding!

The evocative/invocative mode of communication works quite differently, according to Wangerin. In this mode of communication stories are told. Stories are experiential; they create an encounter with the hearer. In this mode the story is the doer and the hearer is the "done to." We participate in the life of a story. As participants in the story we experience the reality of the gospel as it is storied for us. The gospel happens to us. We are there. We are grasped by grace rather than being presented with ideas about grace which we are required to comprehend.

2. Communication In A Post-literate Age

The central concern of this book is to find a form of preaching which will move beyond the kind of preaching shaped by a literate culture; a form of preaching that will speak to a post-literate age. Pierre Babin has worked on this same question from the point of view of Christian communication as a whole. Like McLuhan before him, Babin is concerned with the media massage of our time. His assertion is that the ear predominates in an electronic age in a symbolic sense. The ear, he writes, symbolizes the whole body. The essence of electronic communication is vibration and modulation. "The body organ most sensitive to the vibrating phenomena that surround us is the ear. The ear represents the archetype of perception through vibration. Consequently, because of the violence of auditory and visual vibrations which assail us, because of this electronic universe which supercharges all communication, the whole body, in a manner of speaking, becomes a giant ear. Knowledge then tends to be transmitted effectively through vibrations .... Once again, we see the predominance of the ear and therefore a return to a type of oral culture."[10]

This idea of a return in our world to a world that is like the oral culture is a constantly recurring theme in the literature on communication theory. That means that going forward into new forms of communication might best be served by taking a few steps backward. That's part of the clue to discovering successful patterns of communication in a post-literate age.

Babin contrasts eyes and ears. That is what is new about electronic forms of communication. Both eyes and ears are massaged. The balance of this massage may differ from person to person. Babin works to hold these senses in balance. He believes that the literate culture of the eye and the electronic culture of the ear and eye exist side by side. McLuhan, he tells us, may have pronounced the death of the alphabetic, linear culture too soon. McLuhan was not around to study the computer. Babin is convinced that there are aspects of the computer that reinforce the linear eye massage.[12]

Babin, in his attempt to formulate an approach to Christian communication today advocates what he calls stereo catechesis. "I believe that, in catechesis, the time has finally come for us to function with both hemispheres of the brain. Until the 16th century, catechesis functioned essentially in 'mono 1,' with the right-brain hemisphere predominating. Since Gutenberg and the Council of Trent, it has functioned essentially in 'mono 2,' with the left-brain hemisphere predominating. But these times have passed and, although there are still preponderances, we ought now to function definitively in stereo, both in order to enter into the truth of Christ and to respect human wholeness."[13]

Perhaps we need to think of preaching in our time as stereo preaching. Preaching needs to reach both right and left brain. This might mean that the two forms of preaching that I discussed in the first chapter live today side by side. Preaching shaped by the realities of oral culture and preaching shaped by the realities of writing and print culture will exist simultaneously. In my earlier work, *Telling The Story*, I proposed a category of preaching called Didactic Preaching.[14] This was an earlier attempt on my part to talk about the kind of preaching produced by literate culture. This form of preaching need not die completely in a post-literate world.

I would propose that the kind of preaching shaped by the massage of print is relevant in our culture today in several ways. First of all, there are texts of the Bible that are simply didactic in nature. There are texts that teach and we need not be ashamed to apply the best of our teaching techniques to explain them to our congregations.

Secondly, there will be certain audiences of people who are still very much at home in a literate environment. They will be quite comfortable with a logical presentation of ideas.

Thirdly, there arise certain "teachable moments" in the life of people with whom we communicate. I had this fact brought home to me clearly with a series of sermons on the subject of grief that I preached on my radio program: Lutheran Vespers. The sermons were among the most didactic that I preached in that year. These sermons created a tremendous response in terms of requests. Why did these linear, didactic sermons work so well? Because people were experiencing the power of grief in their lives. They were anxious to have help in understanding the dynamics of their grief.

One word of advice on didactic preaching. When we teach we usually have formulated our ideas in a clear outline. Share that outline with your parishioners by putting it in the bulletin or on an overhead projector. Add this visual sense to your teaching sermon. It will help people remember your points! If our sermon is didactic in form we ought to make use of the best teaching methods available.

Communicating the gospel in our time may require preaching in stereo. I've mentioned the ongoing relevance of didactic preaching. There is an abundance of material that can help with this form of preaching. I want to spend the bulk of my energies seeking to help you with another type of preaching, preaching for a post-literate age. I want to propose a paradigm shift in our preaching. I want to propose that we learn again what our oral ancestors knew. I want to propose that we need to learn to think in story in order to communicate effectively in our time.

I have already indicated that the direction I wish to take is a kind of "back to the future." I have pointed out that communications theorists see many similarities between the post-literate and pre-literate worlds. Walter Ong: "I style the orality of a culture totally untouched by any knowledge of writing or printing, 'primarily orality.' It is 'primary' by contrast with the 'secondary orality' of present-day high-technology culture, in which a new orality is sustained by telephone, radio, television and other electronic devices that depend for their existence and functioning on writing and print."[15]

What Happened To Story?

Again, my major proposal is for a paradigm shift in our concept of preaching. I want to propose that we add to our sermon writing repertoire sermons put together by "thinking in story" alongside our ability to create sermons by "thinking in ideas." In chapter one I hypothesized that preaching in an oral culture would have had certain characteristics. The last point in my characterization was that "thinking in story" was the hermeneutic that controlled the process of communication. The Hebrew world was not a phonetic world. It retained its story character. Jesus Christ was incarnate in this storytelling culture. It was not long, however, before the Christian world of storytelling was replaced by another way of thought. It did not take long in the life of the Christian

58

church, however, until the storytelling character of its life was eclipsed. What happened to preaching as "thinking in story" in the Christian tradition?

Paul Scott Wilson addresses this question in his work: *Imagination of the Heart*. He inquires into the relationship in the early church between story and doctrine as alternative ways of preserving the faith. He recognizes that there is a long held bias in the church against story and in favor of doctrine. He sees the third century C.E. as the turning point. "... the footprints of story are faint and almost disappear while those of doctrine are more clearly defined. Why is it that from the fourth century to the present, narrative has been almost excluded from theology?"[16]

Wilson posits four answers to this question. (1) Narrative came to be identified with the Gnostic heresy. (2) Early Christian Platonists like Clement and Origin introduced philosophy into Christianity effectively cutting Christianity off from its Jewish roots in order to make it more palatable to pagans. (3) When Christianity became the religion of the state it was of utmost importance that the doctrines of the faith be clearly uniform. Doctrine served the church in its fight with heresy. (4) When martyrdom was no longer something to which one could aspire the stories of the martyrs were no longer told.[17]

Wilson goes on to note that about the only stories to survive in Christian literature after this time were Augustine's *Confessions* and the writings of some of the mystics.

Wilson's points documenting the loss of the story category in the early church are very helpful. I believe, however, that he fails to note the most important reason of all for the disappearance of a story hermeneutic. I am convinced that the story category lost out almost immediately when Christianity had to function in the phonetic, literary world of the Greek culture. There was a clash of cultures when Christianity entered Greek soil. Oral culture and literate culture collided. To its credit (!) Christianity was able to transform itself into literate categories and evangelize the Greco-Roman world.

59

Don Wardlaw makes a similar assertion. He notes that the controlling structure of early Christian preaching was narrative. "When the church moved solidly into the Hellenistic world to offer the gospel, however, preaching adopted a discursive style that only now is being seriously reconsidered. In contrast to first-century narrative preaching, reflection became the basic sermon framework in the second century . . . . The subsequent history of preaching, for all its complexity and diversity, bears one remarkable constant: the reflective shape of the sermon. (This is what I call "thinking in ideas.") . . . The Greeks have stolen into homiletical Troy and still reign . . . Preachers have simply been grooved in the apparently timeless assumption that preaching as such seems to mean finding sensible, orderly things to say about scriptural texts, rather than letting those texts say things their own way . . .! Fred Craddock wisely asks, 'Why should the multitude of forms and moods within biblical literature . . . be brought together in one unvarying mold, and that copied from Greek rhetoricians of centuries ago?'"[18]

"Thinking in story" as a frame of sermon design was overtaken by design forms shaped in a different kind of media environment. The oral world gave way to the literate world. "Thinking in story" was replaced by "thinking in idea" as the controlling principle of sermon formation. We live in a time when the literate world of "thinking in idea" is challenged. We live in a "secondary oral" culture. "Thinking in story" as a way of sermon design is one response to the challenge of preaching in a post-literate age.

Why Story?

But why story? That is a legitimate question. Remember please, I present "thinking in story" as one response to the challenge of preaching endemic in the shift from literate to post-literate culture. Other people will propose other responses. I look forward to the contributions of others in this field. But let me defend briefly the question of why story?

1. "Thinking in story" is a valid way of approaching communication of the biblical text because that is the way most biblical texts were stitched together in the first place. The narrative sections of the Bible were stories put into writing by the process of "thinking in story." The author(s) of the old Testament book of Genesis, for example, asked themselves simple questions. Which of the stories shall I tell? In what order should I tell them? The same is true for our gospel writers and for many other portions of the Bible. The authors clearly had theological ends in view. But they did theology by thinking in story.

The historical-critical method of biblical interpretation is a product of literate culture. This form of biblical criticism asks questions about texts as if these texts were always in written form; as if the written form of the texts is the key to understanding. Texts are often studied in isolation from each other as if they have meaning independently of their context. Commentaries that we read for our preaching task still follow this general rule. The text is studied in isolation for its meaning. And the meaning is clearly in the past. When stories became texts they began to be treated as the deposits of timeless truth. Texts point to a world of eternal ideas. The historical critical method tests the documents for trustworthiness. If the document is trustworthy, the ideas can be true.

Only recently has this method begun to give way to other more holistic methods. There are now a few commentaries, that help us see a text as a story told in the midst of many other stories. How does this story relate to the story that precedes it? How does it fit into the whole structure of stories in this gospel or whatever narrative we are examining? These seem to me to be the crucial exegetical questions when we understand that narratives are put together by thinking in story. Exegetical methods that seek to find the ideas of the text will not necessarily help us to be grasped by the power of the narrative as a whole.

61

2. The stories of the Bible invite us to participate in their reality. Note: they invite us to participate in their reality not to understand that reality. I am fundamentally convinced that the story character of most biblical literature is a way of inviting our participation in the reality of God's work with Israel and in Jesus Christ. Stories elicit participation.

"Thinking in story" as a way of sermon design also invites participation. Participating in the reality of the gospel in story form is something quite different than understanding the gospel in idea form. We have heard that the new electronic media involve the participation of far more of our senses. We physically participate in electronic communication. I believe that sermons in story form invite a kind of participation that is an important aspect of our experience as electronically massaged persons.

The fact that we participate in the life of stories means that stories function to bring God's presence into our lives. Stories function as a means of grace. The gospel in story is a happening-reality.

3. Stories work by indirection. Working indirectly they have a chance to break through the cultural filters that work in the heads of those who listen to preaching. The gospel message which we hope to communicate is the word of God's gift of love for sinful humanity. The message that Americans experience in this culture is that you must earn your way. It is very difficult to get past the works righteousness character of this culture in 15-20 minutes of preaching each week!

The telling of biblical stories and of stories which help us to experience biblical stories have a chance to get around these cultural filters. We don't see what is coming in the story. When we do, it is too late. We are hooked by the story. Hopefully, it is the gift character of God's love that has caught us by surprise before we have had the chance to filter that message through our cultural filters which have difficulty understanding the way of freedom and grace. Robert Coles in his book, *The Call of Stories*, gives several examples of how his medical students were able to confront issues through the indirection of stories that they could not confront directly.

62

4. The people in stories come to live in our imagination. Hear how a student in one of Dr. Coles' classes described the reality of a person called Stecher from the trilogy of William Carlos Williams. ". . . to me Stecher is — oh, now, part of me! What do I mean? I mean that he's someone; he's a guy I think of. I picture him and can hear him talking . . . . He's inside us . . . . Williams' words have become my images and sounds, part of me. You don't do that with theories. You don't do that with a system of ideas. You do it with a story, because in a story — oh, like it says in the Bible, the word becomes flesh."[19]

We who communicate the Christian tradition hope that this tradition takes root in those who hear. Traditionally we have thought of filling peoples' heads with ideas. But we can just as well think of filling our peoples' heads with people! In truth this has been going on for a long time. Abraham and Sarah, and Moses and Miriam, and David and Ruth, and Jesus and Mary and a whole host of biblical people do live in the heads of Christian people. They have been "storied" into our heads!

Neil Postman is deeply concerned with the way television overwhelms us with a world of images. He calls it a peek-a-boo world. It is a world filled with disconnected images. One only has to watch two minutes of MTV to understand what Postman means. And how are we to survive in this world which hurls images and information at us at such an incredible pace? One thing we can do is to help fill peoples' heads with biblical people. The people of the Bible can live in our heads helping us sort through the maze of images and information that assaults us. I consider that to be one of the key challenges of preaching today. We need to fill peoples' heads with the people of the Bible!

5. Finally, stories are in sync with the way the electronic media work. Frankly, it is difficult to communicate ideas through the mass media. Mass media seldom attempt to communicate ideas. Mass media almost always works through story. People are accustomed to experiencing reality through story. Sermons that work in story fashion imitate the way television most usually works.

I want to add at this point that stories will work best with people involved deeply in the electronic massage of our culture. The story form of communication is, I believe, an imperative form of communication in terms of reaching those who are part of our culture but outside the church. There will be people who have been inside the church for many years, people who have grown up with literate preaching, who will protest the overuse of story. Each preacher in his/her own setting will have to make a determination about the feasibility and frequency of "thinking in story" sermons.

Characteristics Of Sermons For A Post-literate Age

I have made the point many times that one of the ways forward in terms of preaching in a post-literate age is the way backward. "Back to the future." I am proposing a paradigm shift in preaching from preaching conceived of as "thinking in ideas" to preaching conceived of as "thinking in story." At the end of chapter one I used these terms as the conclusion of a list of the characteristics of oral and literate preaching. I am convinced that many of the other aspects of preaching in an oral culture will need to characterize our sermons in the future. I have listed those characteristics as stitching stories together; making significant use of repetition; using particular stiuations or stories in order to move to universal truth; a tone of conflict — perhaps between God and all those things which work against human life; right brain communication and metaphors of participation. I am convinced that it is out of these characteristics that preaching in our post-literate age should be shaped.

I am also convinced that Neil Postman is wrong in his contention that the Christian faith is so characterized by the serious discourse of the age of typography that it cannot make its case on television without losing its soul and that the dominance of electronic media threaten the very existence of literate Christianity. This is a very serious contention on

Postman's part. I have read countless articles by Christians who agree with Postman; who are frightened by what television is doing to the faith. This usually comes forth in such a way that the church should not attempt to make use of mass media today or it will lose its soul.

I could not disagree more strongly with this assertion! In the first place, the future of Christianity does not depend on the necessity of literate discourse. The biblical faith was handed on for many centuries with very little recourse to literate discourse. It was done by telling stories! Storytelling has been a far more central component in the handing on of the faith than has literate discourse! We must not forget that.

That means, secondly, that we can most certainly make use of electronic means of communication without losing our soul. Telling stories, the fundamental way in which our faith has been passed on from generation to generation, works very well on radio and television. We have a mighty story to tell. We can tell it by relearning the art of telling stories for a new medium of communication. Let's not run from this challenge. We mastered print as a means of communicating the Christian faith. We can master this new world of communication as well.

"Thinking in story" is my primary suggested response for proclaiming the gospel in our electronic world. I will discuss a second suggested form of response to preaching in this age in my final chapter. I believe that we also need to learn how to make more use of the senses of our listeners in the preaching task. This in response to a culture which massages many of our senses simultaneously and causes us to vibrate in response.

Before we deal with multi-sensate preaching we need to take a much longer look at my proposal for "thinking in story." In the next chapter I will deal briefly with a theology for preaching. Following that we will deal with the sources of stories for our preaching and a variety of ways of stitching these stories together into sermonic form.

1. Marshall McLuhan, *The Gutenberg Galaxy* (Toronto, The University of Toronto Press, 1962) p. 172-173.
2. Tony Schwarz, *Media: The Second God* (New York, Random House, 1981) p. 11.
3. *Ibid.,* p. 13.
4. McLuhan, *op. cit.,* p. 302.
5. Walter J. Ong, *The Presence of the Word: Some Prolegomena for Cultural and Religious History* (University of Minnesota Press, Minneapolis, 1981) p. 176.
6. *Ibid.,* p. 9.
7. Marshall McLuhan, *Understanding Media: The Extensions of Man* (New York, McGraw Hill Book Company, 1964) p. 36.
8. *Ibid.,* pp. 272-273.
9. Pierre Babin, *The New Era in Religious Communication* (Minneapolis, Fortress Press, 1991) p. 6.
10. *Ibid.,* pp. 58-59.
11. *Ibid.*
12. *Ibid.,* p. 10.
13. *Ibid.,* p. 187.
14. Richard A. Jensen, *Telling The Story,* (Minneapolis, Augsburg Press, 1980) Chapter 1.
15. Walter Ong, *Orality and Literacy: The Technologizing of the Word,* (London and New York, Methuen, 1982) p. 11 cf. also Marshall McLuhan, *op. cit.,* p. 58: "... the electronic implosion now brings oral and tribal ear-culture to the literate West."
16. Paul Scott Wilson, *Imagination of the Heart: New Understandings in Preaching* (Nashville, Abingdon Press, 1988) p. 155.
17. *Ibid.,* pp. 155-157.
18. Don M. Wardlaw, *Preaching Biblically: Creating Sermons in the Shape of Scripture* (Philadelphia, The Westminster Press, 1983) pp. 11, 12, 13, 15.
19. Robert Coles, The Call of Stories (Boston, Houghton Mifflin Company, 1989) p. 128.

CHAPTER THREE
Toward A Theology
For Preaching

Why do we tell stories at all? Why do we preach? What is the burden of our message? What, in other words, is the theological rationale for the task of proclamation? It is not my intention to develop here a full-blown theology for preaching. That is a task for another time. I do, however, want to speak briefly to the issue. In my reading of the homiletical literature I miss the rationale for preaching most of all. Maybe it is taken for granted that everyone knows why we preach or that people from different traditions will answer this question differently. I do not want to be found guilty of proposing a paradigm shift for the preaching task without at least briefly addressing the issue of the content of our preaching. What follows then are notes toward a theology for preaching.

The Law Always Kills

I cannot and do not wish to disguise the fact that my theological roots reach deeply into the Lutheran tradition. What I wish to say here about the task of preaching lives firmly within that faith heritage. I hope I can present this tradition in such a way that Lutheran readers will nod in recognition and non-Lutheran readers will be stimulated to ongoing thought about the nature of preaching within their own theological frame of reference.

Martin Luther asserted that the true theologian was the one who could rightly distinguish between law and gospel. When Lutherans, including this Lutheran, work at theology we almost always work within the parameters of law and gospel. Protestant theology in general talks about three uses of the law.

The first use of law is usually termed the political or civil use of law. The second use of the law, the spiritual or theological use, is the law as a mirror in which we see our lives; the law as revealer of our sins. The third use of the law is law as a guide for Christian living. There is much debate even among Lutherans whether Luther taught the third use of the law. I do not believe that he did.

Understanding these uses of law will immediately take us to the heart of the nature of preaching. The civil or political use of the law refers to the law written on the heart of every person. "They [the Gentiles] show that what the law requires is written on their hearts . . . ."Romans 2:15. Luther understood that God as Creator had built the law into the life of every living being. The civil use of the law, that is, is not revealed! The civil use of the law is natural, it is written on the heart of every living being.

The function of the civil use of law is to help humankind create a civil society. Since all people bear the law within their being, all people can work to make society a more civil place to live. Preaching on the civil use of the law would call upon people to make use of their rational intelligence in making ethical decisions in life and in working toward a civil society. There is nothing particularly Christian about the civil use of the law. It need not, therefore, occupy too much of our preaching energy. The dialogical nature of the classroom is much better suited for the important discussions of the nature of the way we might best work for an improved civil order.

The theological or spiritual use of the law was for Luther the proper use of the law. The law, that is, reveals to us our sinfulness. "What then should we say? That the law is sin? By no means! Yet, if it had not been for the law, I would not have known sin . . . . Apart from the law sin lies dead. I was once alive apart from the law, but when the commandment came, sin revived and I died, and the very commandment that promised life proved to be death to me (Romans 7:7, 8-10)."

The law always kills! That was Luther's dictum about the spiritual use of the law. The law always leaves me helpless, consigned to wrath, doomed to death. This is the proper use of the law and is therefore the proper use of the law in preaching. To preach the law is to render people helpless in their relationship to God. The law kills us and leaves us dead in the eyes of God.

I've heard a lot of sermons in my life that preached the law. Very, very few of those sermons, however, "killed me." Most law preaching doesn't kill; it just wounds people. When I am wounded by the law my response is that I surely deserve this wound and in the future I vow to improve my life so as not to suffer such wounds any more. When the law only wounds us, it sends us into our own inner resources for the strength to live the good life. The law, that is, directs us for help to the precise cause of our problem. The law directs us to our inner being! Such sermons usually end with a band-aid of grace. Christ will help me, the pastor says. I'll do my best and Christ will do his best and between the two of us we'll get my life shaped up.

On the pattern of Dietrich Bonhoeffer I like to call this kind of band-aid grace "cheap grace." Bonhoeffer was deeply critical of "cheap grace." Grace is cheap if it does not cost much either for me or for God. Cheap grace is the gospel proclaimed when it follows the proclamation of cheap law. Cheap law only wounds the sinner. What the wounded sinner needs is just a little help from God; just a little cheap grace.

Costly law, in contrast to cheap law, really kills. It leaves me without hope in the world. I respond to cheap law with the vow that I will be a better person. I respond to costly law with a deep cry for help. Is there anyone who can rescue me from my bondage to sin and death? The answer is yes. There is one who can forgive my sins. There is one who can raise me from the dead. That one's name is Jesus Christ. It cost Jesus his life to come to my rescue. Christ's grace is costly grace. It cost him his life but it enables him to offer new life, resurrection life, to me in my death-bondage.

Preaching the law ought to be a proclamation of costly law! It ought to be the law that slays sinners and leads them to cry out for help. That kind of law preaching leads always to the preaching of the gospel. There is help! Paul writes to the Galatians that the law is our custodian, the one that brings us to Christ (Galatians 3:24-25). True preaching of the law drives people into the arms of the Savior!

Just one word of caution about preaching the law that kills. Very often the people who fill our pews have already felt the death arrows of the law in their daily life. The law calls upon people to perform. In daily life people are called to perform endlessly on the job, in their families, in their communities. The pressure to perform is relentless. Life so often beats people down. They are painfully aware that they do not measure up. The last thing such persons need when they go to church is to be beaten down even more by the law!

Preaching the law to such people ought to enable them to see that it is indeed the "law of performance," before God and the human family, that has worked in their life. As preachers we need to find ways to preach the good news of the gospel in such a way that it heals the real hurts of people. It doesn't do a lot of good to add new hurts to people's lives through our preaching of the law and then solve the hurts we have created through our preaching of the gospel. The end result is that people have come to our pews burdened by the law and they go home carrying the same burden!

The third use of the law is the law as a guide to Christian living. For Calvin this was the proper use of the law. This marks a radical breach among protestants. Some protestants see the law as God's revealed law for life. Clearly such a law should be preached so that people know how to live! I have already stated my conviction that Martin Luther did not teach the third use of the law in this manner. He did not believe that God revealed the law either to Israel or to Christians as a guide to living! The most radical instance of this is Luther's comments on the law as given to Moses. Luther said, "I keep the commandments which Moses has given, not because Moses gave commandments, but because they have been implanted in me by nature, and Moses agrees exactly with nature etc."[1]

70

Luther believed that the law was natural to every person alive. That's the first use of the law! For Luther, therefore, the law does not need to be revealed. If that is the case then we will need spend little time preaching the law as a guide to life. Here, too, it may be better to deal with such ethical questions about life in discussion forums under the assumption that each person brings unique resources, resources given them by God the Creator, to the discussion.

Preach the law. Preach the costly law. Preach the law that costs sinners their life and brings them to the point that they cry out for a Savior.

The Gospel As Proclamation

Sinners slain by the law long for a word of proclamation. They don't want information about help. That's what too much of literate preaching has done. It has offered the sinner three points about help. Sinners want help! They want to hear a word that sets them free; that forgives their sins; that gives them resurrection life. That's what good preaching does! It gives people life. It announces, proclaims, life. That is the task of preaching.

Luther understood this proclamatory task of preaching very well. He understood that preaching was a living word of life hurled into the dungeon of death. Preaching didn't talk about help. Preaching is help! Fred W. Meuser writes of Luther's understanding of preaching: "Through the spoken word the power and victory of Christ invade life today. Preaching is therefore not only about the saving acts of God. The sermon itself is a saving event."[2]

Luther has a strong theology of the power of God's word and the power of the word of preaching. Christ didn't write anything, Luther said. Writing is not what Christ and the apostles did. They spoke. They preached. "And the gospel should not really be something written, but a spoken word which brought forth the scriptures, as Christ himself did not write anything but only spoke. He called his teaching not scripture but gospel, meaning good news or a proclamation that is spread not by pen but by word of mouth. So we go on and make the gospel into a law book, a teaching of commandments, changing Christ into a Moses, the One who would help us into simply an instructor."[3]

We make the gospel into a law book. What does Luther mean? He means that Christ has come to help sinners. He brings that help to people through his voice and his touch. He announces help. He announces forgiveness. He announces resurrection. Our preaching should likewise consist of such announcements. But, too often, our preaching just talks about the announcements that Christ made. We talk about Christ's announcements as if they are in the past rather than proclaiming them as realities of the present moment of preaching.

Hear Luther again: "When you open the book containing the gospels and read or hear how Christ comes here or there, or how someone is brought to him, you should therein perceive the sermon or the gospel through which he is coming to you, or you are being brought to him. When you see how he works, however, and how he helps everyone to whom he comes or who is brought to him, then rest assured that faith is accomplishing this in you and that he is offering your soul exactly the same sort of help and favor through the gospel. If you pause here and let him do you good, that is, if you believe that he benefits and helps you, then you really have it. Then Christ is yours, presented to you as a gift."[4]

These words of Luther offer us a hermeneutic for coming to the scripture and a way toward preaching. The hermeneutic is simple. As we study the text each week we are to "pause here and let Christ do us good." Christ is active through scripture. That's the work of the Holy Spirit. The Holy Spirit brings Christ off of the pages of the past-tense Bible and makes him present tense in our lives today.

Preaching should participate in this same reality. Preaching should announce words that intend to do good to the hearer. We preach Christ! Our words of preaching become the means for Christ to speak to our congregation. The Holy Spirit takes our words and makes them happen in the lives of the hearers. I have written elsewhere that this means that at the proclamation point of our sermon we need to speak in first or second person, present tense language.[5] I (first person) say to you, your sins are (present tense) forgiven." We speak on Christ's behalf. We don't talk about what Christ said long ago. We don't talk about Christ. We speak for Christ. Christ speaks through us.

It is vitally important with most gospel texts that we at some point in the sermon speak for Christ. You will have discovered what the heart of the text is through your exegetical study. You have paused before the text to let Christ do you good. Speak that heart of the text to the congregation on Christ's behalf as present tense proclamation. This kind of proclamation is worlds removed from preaching that only explains what it was that Christ said and did at some point in the past. Understanding is not the goal. Proclamation is the goal. How that proclamation works itself out in the lives of people is the work of the Holy Spirit.

In a recent book Gerhard Forde has made claims for preaching that precisely parallel my own. His book is titled: *Theology Is For Proclamation*. The title of the book is the book's central argument. Forde is a systematic theologian. Systematic theology, he maintains, has to be for proclamation in a double sense. First, it insists on proclamation. Second, systematic theology recognizes that insistence on preaching is its ultimate purpose.[6]

Forde calls his book something between an essay and an outline of systematic theology. His goal is to show how systematic theology and preaching interact. "I intend to show that both proclamation and systematic theology will be understood and done differently where such correlation is observed and maintained."[7]

His definition of preaching as proclamation is nearly identical to the definition I set forth in *Telling The Story*. Forde: "Proclamation . . . is explicit declaration of the good news,

73

the gospel, the kerygma .... Proclamation belongs to the primary discourse of the church. Systematic theology belongs to its secondary discourse. Primary discourse is the direct declaration of the Word of God.... Secondary discourse, words about God, is reflection on primary discourse. As primary discourse, proclamation ideally is present-tense, first-to-second person unconditional promise authorized by what occurs in Jesus Christ according to the scriptures. The most apt paradigm for such speaking is the absolution...."[8]

In *Telling The Story* I suggested that preaching is the public practice of absolution; the public practice of the Office of the Keys. Preaching, that is, takes the announcement of forgiveness which is uttered in private (which is the practice of the Office of the Keys), and goes public with that announcement! Preaching is a means of grace. It is a sacrament through which the grace of God happens to people. Forde also conceives of preaching as a sacrament: "Proclamation is more like a sacrament than other oral communication such as teaching or informing .... Preaching, to Luther, is pouring Christ into our ears, just as in the sacraments we are baptized into him and he is poured into our mouths. Indeed, preaching is as much a physical activity as baptism or the supper. The proclaimed Word not only explains or informs but it also gives — it ends the old and begins the new, it puts to death and brings to life."[9]

Sacraments use physical means to make Christ's presence real to us. Baptism uses water. The Lord's Supper uses bread and wine. Preaching uses sounded words. I have come to understand in new ways that sounded words also have physical properties. Sounded words leave the body of the speaker and enter physically into our bodies. Through the sounded words of preaching Christ physically enters the bodies of those who hear![10]

Preaching as proclamation lives in the vertical relationship between God and humankind. The biggest problem with such preaching is that it tends to live only in the vertical moment before God. There is at times very little connection between this kind of preaching and the lives we live each day in the horizontal relations of our life. Justification, that is, does not inform God's and our activities of justice in the world. One looks in vain in Forde's work, for example, for any sign of how proclamation moves into the ethical dimension of life.

Forde makes a distinction, based on Luther's *Bondage of the Will,* between our relationship as humans to things above us (the vertical dimension of faith) and our relationship to things below us (the horizontal dimension of faith). He maintains, with Luther, that our human will is bound entirely with respect to things above us. With respect to the things "below us," however, with respect to down to earth realities, we do have free will. It occurs to me that it is just at this point that we ought to engage in ethical conversation. We can talk about ethics in the arena of our free will, in the arena of the "things below."

Forde acknowledges this. He writes: "Luther means that we decide what to do with our money and goods, to come and to go, take what jobs we wish, choose our friends, and so on. I expect we could expand the list even to include such things as morality. We can decide or be persuaded to act morally or immorally."[11] Morality is in the arena of the things that we can decide to do. The bondage of the will that will work in this environment of our decision making is that we will always be bound (this is the bondage of the will!) to make our ethical decision making the ground for our standing before God. Our ethical life, however, is not directed to heaven and to God. Our ethical life is directed to the earth and to our neighbor.

The problem I face in my strong preference for proclamatory preaching, the problem I find with Forde's work as well, is to show how such preaching helps to inform and inspire us to action with reference to the arena of the "things below," the arena of life wherein we do have free will. What are we to do with the new life given to us through the proclamation of the gospel? Can preaching be of no help to us in matters of the ethical life? Is preaching only about the God who establishes a graceful vertical relationship with us?

75

Preaching For Transformed Imagination

One of the most helpful books I have read in this connection is Walter Brueggemann's book, *Finally Comes The Poet*. The title of Brueggemann's book comes from the famous poem, "Leaves of Grass," by Walt Whitman.[12] Brueggemann's concern in this work is that the preaching of the gospel has been flattened out and trivialized. He believes we need to find another way to speak and he submits that poetic speech is the only language worthy of the name preaching. "The poet/prophet is a voice that shatters settled reality and evokes new possibility in the listening assembly. Preaching continues that dangerous, indispensable habit of speech. The poetic speech of text and of sermon is prophetic construal of a world beyond the one taken for granted."[13]

In his work Brueggemann seeks to show the ways in which preaching can be a poetic construal of an alternative world. Brueggemann particularly posits this construal of an alternative world as the way of preaching on the ethical issues of life. Moralism, he asserts, will not move people to new forms of obedience. Moralistic preaching only divides people into those who agree with the preacher and those who disagree. It is better, he suggests, to take on the great ethical problems of our time indirectly. In other words, it is the way of story that is the way for preaching in the horizontal realm. He quotes Paul Ricoeur to the effect that obedience follows imagination.

Brueggemann comments on Ricoeur's dictum as follows: "Our obedience will not venture far beyond or run risks beyond our imagined world. If we wish to have transformed obedience ... then we must be summoned to an alternative imagination, in order that we may imagine the world and ourselves differently. The link of obedience to imagination suggests that the toughness of ethics depends on poetic, artistic speech as the only speech that can evoke transformed listening."[14]

Just one more word from Brueggemann. He writes that preaching ought to be an event in transformed imagination.

"The new conversation, on which our very lives depend, requires a poet and not a moralist. Because finally church people are like other people; we are not changed by new rules. The deep places in our lives — places of resistance and embrace — are not ultimately reached by instruction. Those places of resistance and embrace are reached only by stories, by images, metaphors and phrases that line out the world differently, apart from our fear and hurt."[15]

Places of ethical resistance in the human heart are reached only by stories! In matters of the "things below," in the matters of the horizontal living out of life, we as preachers will best enable change in our listeners by "thinking in story." The issue is, what stories can we tell? What stories can we tell to enable transformed obedience? What stories can we tell to picture an alternative world? What stories can we tell to move the imagination of our listeners to new planes of ethical endeavor?

Brueggemann's book offers some excellent examples. Motivated directly by Brueggemann I took a new look at the book of Daniel in this regard. As I will say in the next chapter, I believe more and more that the first place we ought to turn for stories to tell is the Bible! My new look at Daniel surprised me. I had learned all the information that modern scholarship had taught with regard to the book of the "prophet" Daniel. I had learned that the Book of Daniel is not what it purports to be on the surface of things. It purports to take place in Babylon during the time of the exile of Israel in Babylon. Actually it was written hundreds of years after the Babylonian exile to speak to a new situation where foreign culture threatened to swamp Israel's faith. These "old" stories are told for a new situation of cultural coercion.

Thus I had been taught. What no one had ever bothered to help me do, however, was to recover the first six chapters of Daniel as powerful stories of the preservation of faith in the light of a culture that was inimical to faithfulness to Yahweh. In my new reading I rediscovered Daniel as story! In my rediscovery I could suddenly see that these stories of Daniel speak a powerful word to our own day when our culture threatens to usurp our faith.

How shall we live our lives as Christian people in the light of a culture that threatens to swamp us? I propose that one way we might deal with this question is to seek to transform our people's imagination, paint for them an alternative vision, by telling again some of the stories of Daniel. Daniel and his friends were taken into exile by the Babylonians. They lived together in a strange land; a land that would test their faith.

The first test of their faith was a test of consumption. The king assigned them a daily portion of the rich food that the king ate. But Daniel said "No." By the laws of Israel this food was unclean. Daniel refused to eat.

Consumption. That was the first test that a foreign culture imposed upon Daniel. I would submit that consumption is a test of faith in our culture as well. You know the statistics on the over consumption of America of the world's energy and goods. Our patterns of consumption actually create injustice in the world.

Daniel would not consume! He asked those charged with his care not to feed him the rich food of Babylon. The chief of the eunuchs was troubled by Daniel's request. "If I do what you ask," he said to Daniel, "and you appear to be in poorer condition than others of your own age, I will be in real trouble. I could lose my head over something like this."

Daniel challenged the chief of the eunuchs. "Test your servants for ten days," Daniel said, "let us be given vegetables to eat and water the drink. Then let our appearance and the appearance of the youths who eat the king's rich food be observed by you . . . (Daniel 1:12-13)." Daniel took a risk of faith. He risked his life rather than buy into the patterns of consumption of a culture that was alien to his faith.

The experiment was carried out. For 10 days Daniel and his friends did not consume the culture's fare. When the 10 days were over the steward checked out the appearance of the Israelite youths in training. To his great surprise Daniel and his friends were "better in appearance and fatter in flesh" than all the youths who ate the king's rich food. Daniel obeyed God rather than the demands of this alien culture. Daniel did not sell out to the culture! And he was better off!

What might happen to us if we refused the fare of our culture for 10 days or more? What might happen to us if we turned our back on the consumption patterns of our society? After 10 days would we, like Daniel, be in better condition than those who have sold their soul for the goods of our culture?

This story of Daniel is a story for transformed imagination. It paints a picture of another reality. It invites us to a transformed imagination and obedience as we live our lives in a consumption addicted society.

There are other such stories in Daniel. In chapter three the issue is gold! Nebuchadnezzar built a giant image of gold in the land and ordered all to fall down and worship before it. An image of gold to worship. I hardly think I need to explain to you the relevance of this story in our culture.

Shadrach, Meshach and Abednego, of course, would not worship the gold. The king, therefore, threw them into a fire that was seven times hotter than normal! It was so hot that the men who were to throw them into the fire were consumed by it. But Shadrach, Meshach and Abednego were not harmed. King Nebuchadnezzar looked down upon them and was stunned by what he saw. The men were alive and walking around in the fire. There was a mysterious fourth man walking with them whom Nebuchadnezzar said had the appearance like a son of the gods [See Daniel 3:25]. Might a son of the gods walk with us in our refusal to bow down to the images of gold in our culture?

The final story from the book of Daniel that speaks with such relevance to our culture is the story told in Daniel 4. It's a story about patriotism and pride. It's a story about the role that a nation plays in human affairs. It's a story about the dangers of misplaced pride in the nation. I preached on this text from Daniel during the patriotic aftermath of the war in the Persian Gulf in 1991. This sermon is included at the end of this chapter. I think it is a story that can be told to help

79

transform the imagination of the listeners as they struggle with the proper role of love of nation in human affairs.

Telling Stories Of Participation And Imagination

My paradigm for preaching is "thinking in story." I am firmly convinced that we need to learn how to think in story as one of the ways we put sermons together. As I have indicated in chapter one and two these stories ought to be stories that are metaphors of participation, not metaphors of illustration. Stories that are metaphors of illustration are stories that are told to illustrate the point we have made about law, gospel and transformed imagination. We would explain to our hearers how the law kills and then tell a story to illustrate our point. We would explain to our hearers how the gospel heals and then tell a story to illustrate our point. In this model stories are told to explain ideas.

I propose a different model. I propose that we tell stories as metaphors of participation. We tell stories in which the law works to convict a person of sin. Our hope in telling such a story is that people will participate in the life of the story. Our hope is that we will not have to explain how the law works. Our hope is that people will experience the work of the law as they participate in the story(s) we tell.

The same is true for the preaching of the gospel. We tell stories in which God's love for sinful humanity happens. People are forgiven and healed and raised to a new life. Our hope is that as people participate in stories of gospel events, the gospel will also happen to them. In this instance the gospel works indirectly. It is as we experience the gospel happening in the life of the story that the gospel also happens to us.

The gospel, of course, can also be proclaimed directly. After we have told our gospel-event stories we might turn to the congregation, so to speak, and announce Jesus' gospel word to them in first or second person, present tense language. The listener hears and experiences the gospel event indirectly through the medium of the story and/or directly through the mouth of the preacher who speaks for Jesus.

Ethical concerns as well may best be dealt with indirectly through the listeners' participation in a story which seeks to transform the imagination and paint an alternative world of ethical possibility. People do need down-to-earth help in making the difficult ethical decisions that confront us in our time. I close this chapter with a sermon on the book of Daniel which seeks to transform the human imagination in its understanding of the relationship between the sovereignty of God and the sovereignty of nations.

Sermon: "The Most High Sovereign"
Daniel 4
(This sermon was originally preached on Lutheran Vespers on June 2, 1991.)

Patriotism lives! The victory of coalition forces over Iraq in the early months of 1991 seems to have given our pride back to us as a nation. On one occasion President Bush said, "We've finally licked this Vietnam thing." On another occasion he said, "This war has helped America rediscover itself." The President has ordered that our 4th of July celebrations welcome our troops and fly the flag high. America is standing tall again. We're clearly the number one nation in the world — at least in terms of our military might. I don't remember such excitement in our nation since I was a boy — since the end of World War II.

Patriotism lives! We've heard it in new songs on the radio. We've seen a Whitney Houston rendition of our National Anthem, sung at the Super Bowl, become a hit on the music charts. I watched a religious television program where the song after the sermon was the National Anthem sung in front of a large American flag. The stripes on the flag were about three feet wide. It was huge! Patriotism lives! We're proud of our nation. We're proud to be Americans.

Where does the voice of the church fit in all of this celebration of national pride? I've just indicated that one religious expression that I saw glorified the flag. How are Christians to relate to all of this national pride? How are you and I to relate to the new found glory of our nation?

Let me tell you a story from the Old Testament book of Daniel. I find this Old Testament book able to speak in pardoxical relevance to the issue of national pride. It is paradoxical because the nation in charge of events in the book of Daniel is Babylon of old — a nation that was situated pretty much where modern day Iraq is today. In the time of Daniel Babylon, modern day Iraq, was the number one nation in the world. Babylon stood tall. Babylon was proud of its achievements. The story told in Daniel chapter 4 tells us how pride and nationhood belong together.

King Nebuchadnezzar of Babylon was riding high. As the world's dominant power he sent out a decree to all the peoples, nations and languages that dwelt on the earth. The decree went like this: "May you have abundant prosperity! The signs and wonders that the Most High God has worked for me I am pleased to recount. How great are his signs, how mighty his wonders. His kingdom is an everlasting kingdom, and his sovereignty is from generation to generation (Daniel 4:1-3)."

Sounds good doesn't it! It sounds like Nebuchadnezzar is really giving the glory to the Most High God. The Most High God is the book-of-Daniel's-expression for the God that the Israelites worshiped. This decree fools you for a minute. All the right words are there. But what do you think the Israelites thought when they heard this decree from the king of the nation that had conquered them? Do you think for a minute that they believed that Nebuchadnezzar really served the Most High God with all his heart, soul, strength and mind? No way! They knew the truth about Nebuchadnezzar. They knew that his pride was not in their God. They knew Nebuchadnezzar's fine sounding phrases couldn't cover the fact that Nebuchadnezzar's pride was really in himself and the accomplishments of his nation.

In verse 4 of chapter 4 the real story begins. King Nebuchadnezzar was prospering in his palace. But right there in the security of his palace, in the security of all his accomplishments, he had a dream that filled him with anxiety. When we hear about this dream we, the readers of this story, know what the Israelites who first heard this story knew: God is quietly at work in this story. King Nebuchadnezzar had a dream that alarmed him.

Nebuchadnezzar wanted to know the meaning of his dream; he wanted to get at the roots of his fear. So he called to himself all the magicians and enchanters and the astrologers to help him interpret the dream. But no one, no one in the whole of this mighty kingdom, no one in the mighty land of Babylon, could interpret his dream. No one, that is, knew the language of the Most High God!

So Nebuchadnezzar had to send for a man of Israel, a man, as he put it, "who is endowed with a spirit of the holy gods (Daniel 4:8)." King Nebuchadnezzar sent for Daniel and told him his dream. This is the dream.

Upon my bed this is what I saw;
there was a tree at the center of the earth,
*   and its height was great.*
The tree grew great and strong,
*   Its top reached to heaven,*
*   and it was visible to the ends of the whole earth.*
Its foliage was beautiful,
*   its fruit abundant,*
*   and it provided food for all.*
The animals of the field found shade under it,
the birds of the air nested in its branches,
and from it all living beings were fed.
I continued looking, in the visions of my head as I lay
in bed, and there was a holy watcher, coming down from
heaven. He cried aloud and said:
"Cut down the tree and chop off its branches,
strip off its foliage and scatter its fruit.
Let the animals flee from beneath it
and the birds from its branches.

83

But leave its stump and roots in the ground,
with a band of iron and bronze,
in the tender grass of the field.
Let him be bathed with the dew of heaven,
and let his lot be with the animals of the field
in the grass of the earth.
Let his mind be changed from that of a human,
and let the mind of an animal be given to him.
And let seven times pass over him.
The sentence is rendered by decree of the watchers,
the decision is given by order of the holy ones,
in order that all who live may know
that the Most High is sovereign over the kingdom of
mortals;
he gives it to whom he will
and sets over it the lowliest of human beings."

— Daniel 4:10-17

"That's my dream" Nebuchadnezzar said to Daniel. "No one has been able to interpret it. But you are endowed with the 'spirit of the holy gods.' Tell me the meaning."

Daniel was terrified by the dream. He told Nebuchadnezzar that he hoped the dream and its interpretation were meant for the king's enemies. "The tree that you saw," Daniel began, "the tree that grew great and strong, the tree whose top reached into the heavens, — it is you O king! You have grown great and strong. Your greatness reaches the heavens. Your sovereignty reaches to the ends of the earth."

We pick up clues right away in Daniel's interpretation. The king of Babylon reaches into the heavens. That always seems to be the sin of Babel in the Old Testament. In Genesis 11 the people of Babel tried to build a tower to the heavens so that they could make a name for themselves. Building a tower to the heavens is an expression of human pride. Babylon and pride seem to go together. In our story it is the pride of the king of Babylon, the pride of Nebuchadnezzar, that is the problem.

Daniel continued with his interpretation. Nebuchadnezzar's greatness, the greatness of a tree reaching the heavens, is about to come to an end says Daniel. The watcher and the holy one from heaven announce the verdict upon the tree, that is, upon the King of Babylon. "Cut down the tree and destroy it;" they say, "but leave its stump and roots in the ground ... (v. 23)." "This means, O King," Daniel says, "that the decree of the Most High has come upon you: You shall be driven away from human society, and your dwelling shall be with the wild animals (v. 25)." The Most High is teaching the King of Babylon a lesson. "You must learn, O King," Daniel continues, "that the Most High has sovereignty over the kingdom of mortals, and gives it to whom he will .... your kingdom shall be established for you from the time that you learn that Heaven is sovereign (v. 26)." Heaven is to be sovereign over Babylon! Babylon is not to be sovereign over heaven!

Daniel then becomes very direct with the king. "You must atone for your sins," Daniel tells Nebuchadnezzar. "You must replace your sins with righteousness; you must replace your iniquities with mercy to the oppressed (v. 27)."

But Nebuchadnezzar would not listen to Daniel. The world's greatest nation would not listen to the Most High God. Nebuchadnezzar went about his tasks as before. One day, about a year after Daniel interpreted his dream for him, the pride-filled king was walking on the roof of the royal palace. With great pride he looked out over the city he had built. He said, "Is this not magnificent Babylon, which I have built as a royal capital by my mighty power and for my glorious majesty (v. 30)?"

A voice from heaven answered Nebuchadnezzar. "The kingdom has departed from you (v. 31)." That's what the voice said. "You shall be driven away from human society, and your dwelling shall be with the animals of the field. You shall be made to eat grass like oxen, and seven times shall pass over you until you have learned that the Most High has sovereignty over the kingdom of mortals and gives it to whom he will (v. 32)."

And, immediately, Daniel's words concerning Nebuchadnezzar's future came to pass. When the king's time of punishment was over, Nebuchadnezzar had learned his lesson. His reason returned to him. He blessed and praised the Most High God. He said:

> *"I blessed the Most High,*
> *and praised and honored the one who lives forever.*
> *For his sovereignty is an everlasting sovereignty,*
> *and his kingdom endures from generation to generation.*
> *All the inhabitants of the earth are accounted as nothing,*
> *and he does what he wills with the host of heaven*
> *and the inhabitants of the earth.*
> *There is no one who can stay God's hand*
> *or say to him, 'What are you doing?' "*
>
> — Daniel 4:34-35

The storyteller then tells us that King Nebuchadnezzar's reason returned to him. His majesty and splendor were also restored to him. His sovereignty was reestablished. Nebuchadnezzar's final words in this story are that he now honors the King of heaven who is able to bring low those who walk in pride (v. 37)!

The theme of this story is not difficult to discover. It is repeated in verses 17, 25 and 32. The theme is that the Most High God is sovereign over the kingdom of mortals. The Most High God is sovereign over Babylon. The Most High God is sovereign over the USA. The Most High God is sovereign over every nation on earth. Nations are to serve the Most High God and only the Most High God. This alone is to be their pride.

National boundaries and national pride helps to unite groups of people. At the same time, however, it is precisely national pride that shatters and divides the global human family today. We have only to see what is happening today in Russia and Eastern Europe and Africa and Northern Ireland to see how nationalism works to divide people from people. Division! That's what happens when our pride as a nation is in ourselves. Our pride is only to be pride in the Most High God.

The Most High God is sovereign over every mortal kingdom. This God calls every nation to repentance. This God calls every nation to turn from its sin. This God calls every nation to practice righteousness. This God calls every nation to work in mercy for the oppressed. That was the form of repentance that Daniel called for from King Nebuchadnezzar. He called upon the king to atone for his iniquities with mercy to the oppressed (Daniel 4:27).

When all the world's oppressed peoples are set free, then all peoples in all nations will know that they are number one — number one in the eyes of the Most High God.

When all the world's oppressed peoples are set free, then all peoples in all nations will take pride in God alone.

When all the world's oppressed peoples are set free, then all peoples in all nations will know that the Most High God is truly sovereign over every mortal nation. Amen.

---

1. Helmut T. Lehmann, gen. ed., *Luther's Works,* 54 vols., vol. 35, *Word and Sacrament I,* ed. E. Theodore Bachmann (Philadelphia: Muhlenberg, 1960) p. 168.
2. Fred W. Meuser, *Luther The Preacher* (Minneapolis, Augsburg Publishing House, 1983), p. 26.
3. Lehmann, *op. cit.,* p. 123.
4. Helmut T. Lehmann, gen. ed., *Luther's Works,* 54 vols., vol. 36, *Word and Sacrament II,* ed. Abdel Ross Wentz (Philadelphia: Muhlenberg, 1960) p. 121.
5. Richard A. Jensen, *Telling The Story: Variety and Imagination in Preaching* (Minneapolis, Augsburg Publishing, 1980) p. 79.
6. Gerhard O. Forde, *Theology Is For Proclamation* (Minneapolis, Fortress Press, 1990) p. vii.
7. *Ibid.,* p. 5.
8. *Ibid.,* pp. 1-2.
9. *Ibid.,* pp. 147, 149.
10. Martin Luther once said: "Now see, as I have said, how much the poor bodily voice is able to do. First of all it brings the whole Christ to the ears; then it brings him into the hearts of all who listen and believe." Lehman, *ibid.,* pp. 340-341.
11. Forde, *op. cit.,* p. 45.

12. After the seas are cross'd (as they seem already cross'd / After the great captains and engineers have accomplish'd their work, / After the noble inventors, after the scientists, the chemist, the geologist, ethnologist, / Finally shall come the poet worthy of that name, / The true son of God shall come singing his songs. ... from Walter Brueggemann, *(Finally Comes The Poet: Daring Speech for Proclamation* (Minneapolis, Fortress Press, 1989), frontpiece.

13. *Ibid.,* p. 4.

14. *Ibid.,* p. 85.

15. *Ibid.,* pp. 109-110.

CHAPTER FOUR
Sources Of Stories

We now turn our attention to the very practical matter of determining how we might learn to "think in story." In his book titled, *Imagination of the Heart: New Understandings in Preaching,* Paul Scott Wilson gives this helpful definition of story. Story, he writes, is a ". . . sequence of events or images that employs plot, character and emotion. Plot gives it direction; character gives it humanity; and emotion gives it people in relationship."[1] When we are looking for stories to tell, therefore, we are looking for that right combination of plot, character and emotion that we can tell in order that the heart of the biblical text for the day might come alive in the lives of our listeners.

I have lectured to many pastors' groups on this approach to the task of preaching. On one occasion an excellent former student of mine said at the end of the day: "What you are saying sounds simple but I think you are trying to move us to a whole new way of thinking. You are asking us to learn a new language of discourse." I hadn't thought of it that way until this pastor raised the issue. I think this pastor was right. For some people learning to "think in story" is like learning a new language.

I would propose that it is a new language that we can all learn. Once the importance of "thinking in story" had seized my imagination I set out to teach myself to think in this new language. It can be done! One of the things we must do in learning this mode of thought is to recognize where we might turn for the source of stories. What stories can we tell? The purpose of this chapter is to help you identify possible sources of story. There is nothing new here. The sources of story are quite obvious once we set our minds to the task.

1. The Bible

The first and most obvious source of stories is the Bible itself. Let me say it very simply: we can tell Bible stories!

In my earlier work on sermonic storytelling I concentrated on telling stories other than biblical stories as a way of bringing people to the biblical story from a fresh perspective in order that the biblical text might speak in new ways. I was always clear that non-biblical stories were told in the service of texts of scripture.[2] We don't tell stories for their own sake. We tell stories always in the service of texts.

Mark Ellingsen writes of the preaching task from the background of what is called "narrative theology."[3] From his perspective the use of non-biblical stories that I advocated in my earlier work is deeply problematic. His viewpoint is an important and helpful critique which I would like to share briefly with you.

Ellingsen begins with definitions. He demarcates the difference between story theology or story preaching on the one hand, and biblical narrative or narrative theology on the other hand. He identifies himself as an advocate for biblical narrative theology. His book is an attempt to define biblical narrative theology and show its homiletical implications.[4]

Biblical narrative theology, according to Ellingsen, means telling and re-telling the stories of the Bible. Story-type preachers, on the other hand, (and he includes my work under this heading) tell stories from outside the world of the Bible in order to enhance the message of the biblical text. Speaking on behalf of biblical narrative theology, Ellingsen puts the case this way: ". . . when preaching becomes understood as the task of narrating the biblical account, scripture effectively functions as its own interpreter. It interprets itself insofar as such preaching rejects the imposition of extraneous categories upon itself, and it allows its narratives to speak for themselves . . . . in my model, the canonical text . . . is deemed authoritative . . . because it alone bears witness to the full history of revelation. . . ."[5]

Ellingsen, therefore, is highly skeptical of using stories from outside the canon to help understand or grasp the canon of scripture. He is intent on the fact that the biblical world is an other world from our world. Stories from the biblical world

90

interpret our world but stories from our world ought not be used to make connections to the biblical world. He talks about the world of biblical narrative as a world unto itself. Questions of historicity regarding these stories, for example, are not germane. The biblical world should be treated as realistic narrative. The narrative is true! "Questions of truth, relevance and modern meaning will take care of themselves because these stories have a way of transforming the lives of those who hear them."[6]

This view of the Bible as realistic narrative makes strong claims on the Bible's power to present to us the presence of God. Ellingsen uses words such as "overwhelm" and "tyrannical" in a positive sense to indicate the way that the Bible has power over our lives. I do not like the use of this abusive language to describe the way the Bible functions but I have always believed that the Bible is a means of God's presence to our lives. The Bible, as Lutherans say it, is a means of grace. In Ellingsen's terms, we are to treat the biblical story as a piece of literature which functions the way a novel functions. Something happens to us when we read a novel. God happens to us when we are confronted with biblical narrative!

Ellingsen's approach strikes me as both useful and problematic. The problem is his separation of the world of the Bible from the world of ordinary life. With one eye on Paul Tillich he rejects any sort of correlation between the human world and the biblical world. We cannot, therefore, tell stories from the normal human world as a way of moving towards the biblical story. He believes that any attempt to use the normal human world in this way must be based on some sort of structuralist presuppositions which he criticizes.

I believe we can use non-biblical stories as a way towards the biblical text and as a way of helping the biblical text speak to our world today. Theologically I base my conviction on the First Article of the Creed. "I believe in God the Father almighty, creator of heaven and earth." This world, fallen though it be, is God's created world. When God chose to be revealed to us God used the stuff of this creation as God's means of presence. The world of the Bible is not some other world! The world of the Bible is this world in which we live. God meets us in this world. God's revelation of grace, mercy and forgiveness comes to the people of this world through the stuff of this world. God's world of revelation is not through some other world called the Bible. God's revelation in Jesus Christ is correlated precisely with human needs. God's work in Christ is the answer to the problems of life as we experience it. The gospel of God's revelation is a response to the way the law has worked in our lives. We can, therefore, tell human stories which lead in correlative fashion to a longing to hear the good news story of God.

I want to affirm much of what Ellingsen asserts about the power of biblical narrative. I think that the Bible is by far our most important source of stories as we learn to "think in story." These stories that took place in our world are the unique source and norm of our Christian life and faith. These stories do have power over us. They are unique means of grace. They speak to human need with amazing relevance. In this respect I have made a significant movement since the publication of my first work on preaching. I did deal in that work primarily with non-biblical stories as a means of opening up revelatory aspects of the biblical stories. I am much more prone now to simply tell and re-tell the stories of the Bible. I have fallen in love with the Bible all over again!

Falling in love with the Bible all over again was not easy! In the last chapter I related how I had to somehow get by the historical-critical tools of scholarship in order to discover the power of a book like Daniel as story! The historical-critical method was a product of literate culture. It treated the biblical documents as written records. In the process, the story character of these documents was temporarily subverted. Frankly, we live in a wonderful new age wherein we are re-discovering the incredible possibilities of the Bible as story. If you have not as yet made this re-discovery I invite your wholehearted participation in the story world of the Bible.

Be a child again! Let these stories work their way with you. Having worked their way with you, tell them to your congregation in living color! These stories have unique power to touch human lives.

Paul Scott Wilson asserts that new approaches to scripture are very much dependent on an understanding of contemporary art. He cites Thomas H. Troeger to the effect that he was warned as a future teacher of English literature never to read a critic on a poem before reading and living with the text for himself![7] That is excellent advice for those of us who work with scripture as well. Hold off on the commentaries for a while! Read the text. Read it in its context! Walk around the story. Try it on for size. How does it feel? What is going on? Then, and only then, take the commentaries off the shelf. Experience the biblical narrative first as story. Re-create the text as story for your congregation. It's the best material we have at our disposal! Thinking in story begins with the biblical story.

In his work titled, *The Living Word,* Gustaf Wingren set forth a powerful conception of the task of preaching. He saw the Bible as setting forth an ordinary, factual history filled with conflict between the way of God and the way of evil powers. That conflict, he says, does not end with the last book of the Bible. The conflict still goes on. Preaching, he writes, is the present stage of God's redemptive action in history. In other words, it is in and through the task of preaching that God carries on the conflict with evil powers in our world today. "To preach or to hear someone preach is to take one's place within the long chain of Biblical acts . . . ." God acts today through our preaching. God's conflict with all the forces arrayed against life will come to an end only when preaching comes to an end. Preaching comes to an end with the dawn of the eschaton.[8]

We tell the biblical stories as a way of taking our place in the long chain of biblical acts! God acted in history. God continues to act among us through the event of preaching. The stories we tell are the means whereby the salvation that comes from God through Jesus Christ comes to people today. This is the work of the Holy Spirit. The Holy Spirit works in, with and under the stories of our God in order to bring salvation as a present tense reality into the lives of people today.

Thinking in biblical story alerts us to new ways of doing biblical exegesis. Exegesis has traditionally been taught as primarily a vertical exercise. By vertical I mean that we as exegetes are called upon to dig vertically into the depths of the text. Much of this vertical exegesis treats the text as an isolated phenomenon. We take this text with just these few verses and plumb the depth that is there. "Vertical" exegesis makes the assumption that each text is a meaning-world unto itself . . . a highly problematic assumption!

I want to propose that our exegesis begin as a horizontal endeavor. When dealing with a gospel text I believe our first question ought to be a question of why Mark or Luke told just this story in just this sequence. Our gospel writers thought in story. They had many stories available to them. They figured out which stories to tell and in what order to tell them in order to communicate the reality of Jesus of Nazareth to a particular audience. Why this story after the one that precedes or before the one that follows? How does this story fit into the overall framework of this gospel's story? Gospel stories are always stories in context. There are an increasing number of works available in New Testament studies that deal with the story character of our gospels. I commend them to you. Catching the flow of the story can help us avoid being "pericoped" to death. The pericopes that lay before us each week so easily encourage us to study the text in isolation from the overarching story. Text selections for the pericope system skip all around in a given biblical book. It is almost impossible to catch the flow of Matthew's story, for example, from the sequence of pericope texts that are assigned. "Thinking in story" as we work with these pericopes will help keep our listeners apprised of the story character of the biblical material before us.

There is another problem with the pericope system. The pericopes appointed Sunday by Sunday leave out much material between texts. The pericope system often does a hatchet job on the story as a whole. When the gospel for a given Sunday skips a chapter or two in the gospel from which it is taken it is sometimes imperative that we re-story the text for the day. It may be that we simply must tell some of the stories that have been left out of the pericope system in order to set today's story in its proper perspective.

I preached a series of sermons on Lutheran Vespers on the Lord's Prayer. I relate this to you as an example of thinking in biblical story for the construction of the sermon. First, I divided the Lord's Prayer into its several petitions. My treatment of each petition was very simple. I searched the scripture for stories that would throw light on each petition. On the petition, "forgive us our sins as we forgive those who sin against us," I told two parables that Jesus told. I told, first, the story of the Prodigal Son. The Prodigal Son came to the realization that he needed to be forgiven in order to return to his father's home. He prepared a prayer of forgiveness to say to his father. This petition of the Lord's Prayer indicates that each and every one of us is like the Prodigal Son. We come before our God each day with a petition asking for forgiveness of our sins.

The second parable I told in conjunction with this petition of the Lord's Prayer was the story of the king who wished to settle accounts with his slaves. The first slave was forgiven much by his master. But when his fellow slave asked forgiveness from him the first slave would not forgive him. The Lord summoned the wicked slave and said: "I forgave you all that debt because you pleaded with me. Should you not have had mercy on your fellow slave, as I had mercy on you (Matthew 18:32-33)?" This parable of Jesus helps us understand the second part of this petition of the Lord's Prayer that says we are to forgive others as we have been forgiven by God.

Each sermon on the Lord's Prayer followed this format. I put this series of sermons together by thinking in biblical story. The response to this simple biblical approach to the Lord's Prayer was one of the best responses we have ever had at Lutheran Vespers to a series of sermons. Biblical stories undergirding the petitions of the Lord's Prayer opened new avenues of understanding for the listeners. Quite frankly, I was surprised at the response to this simple form of sermon construction.

Our literate tradition trained us to find the ideas in the Bible and to shape them in logical ways for the preaching task. Most of you reading this work will have learned how to use scripture as the source of the ideas you wish to inculcate into the life of your people. There is another possibility. It is certainly a legitimate task to seek to fill the heads of those with whom we communicate with ideas. We can also fill their heads with people! We can tell biblical stories in such a way that the characters of the Bible come to live in the hearts and minds of our listeners. I want to assert again, in the strongest terms possible, that filling peoples' heads with people is every bit as valuable as filling their heads with ideas. Telling biblical stories will accomplish this very important task. One of the ways that the life of Christ can be formed within us is the way of biblical characters living within our consciousness.

Preaching and worship go together. I want to make two comments about the use of the Bible in our worship life. First, the reading of the lectionary each Sunday. This is common in most churches. At some point in the service biblical texts are read. By and large the presentation of scripture has fallen totally under the control of literate culture. In most of the congregations that I visit someone is appointed to read the lessons and the members of the congregations have printed copies in hand in order to follow the text. There is nothing particularly wrong with this arrangement. I do want to note that this way of presenting the texts of scripture is a completely literate experience. The reader reads. The congregation reads along.

We live, however, in a post-literate culture. There would be other ways in which the lessons could be presented. I want to recommend the possibility of oral recitation. Oral recitation is based on the premise that the reader doesn't read and the congregation has no written text in hand. The text, perhaps just the gospel for the day, is recited from memory.

My first experience with oral recitation of scripture came when I attended a workshop on biblical storytelling conducted by Thomas Boomershine. This workshop left a powerful impression within my spirit. The highlight of the event was the final evening. Our assignment was simple. Each one of the nearly 20 participants was to recite from memory a Bible story that had meaning for his or her life. When the time came we gathered on the lawn of the retreat center and took turns with our oral recitation of scripture. There is no way that I can effectively communicate to you the power of that experience. It lasted for two hours. One person after another simply recited a biblical story. It seemed to me that it lasted about 10 minutes! I was transfixed by these Bible stories told as living proclamation. I experienced the power of the Bible as a means of grace in a way that I had not thought possible.

Thomas Boomershine has written a book which lays out the rationale for biblical storytelling titled: *Story Journey: An Invitation to the Gospel as Storytelling.* [9] The book is also a practical guide for learning how to master the art of storytelling. I commend this book to you most highly and urge you to consider oral recitation as an occasional or regular way of communication of one or more of the texts for Sunday.

If I were a parish pastor I would form in my congregation a biblical storytelling group. We would meet each week to learn to tell biblical stories. Out of this group would come the lectors for the Sunday morning service. Out of this group might also come persons who would make hospital calls and/or evangelism calls on behalf of the congregation. These callers would have many biblical stories tucked away in their memory bank that they could recite during the course of their various calls.

Secondly, a comment about children's sermons. I believe that children's sermons would be an ideal time to tell Bible stories. We ought to tell stories that fit in with the greater structure of the sermon for the day. Using the time of the children's sermon as an occasion for telling Bible stories is an excellent way of filling the heads of both young and old with the characters of our Holy Bible.

I propose, therefore, that thinking in story around a particular biblical text begins with thinking in biblical story. We look for other biblical stories we can tell or retell in association with the text for the day that will help bring that text to life.

2. Autobiography

A second source of stories for preaching are the stories that come out of our own life. Oftentimes there is an event in our life that makes for just the right story to tell. We need to be attentive to the story of our own life. This is the story we know best!

The use of autobiographical material in preaching has had a complex history. It was not too long ago that the common advice was that we ought never to make use of personal stories in preaching. This advice came forth from a situation where personal stories were used inappropriately. There are certainly ways in which our stories of self can be used in an inappropriate manner. There can be too much of our self in our preaching. The listeners wonder when they come to church what aspect of our life we will talk about this Sunday. When that happens, we have gone too far. The stories we tell cannot continually revolve around our self and our own private world. Richard L. Thulin of the Lutheran Theological Seminary at Gettysburg, Pennsylvania, has written a very helpful guide for the use of autobiography in preaching. His book is titled: The "I" Of The Sermon.[10] His book deals specifically with the use of first-person singular narrative as a vehicle for the proclamation of God's Word. He gives us a helpful chart concerning the various levels of use of self in preaching. He indicates that we can refer to our selves in the form of an illustration, a reminiscence, a confession and a more complete self-portrayal.[11] Each succeeding category will call for more detail in the personal story. Thulin is most interested in the fullest use of personal story: story as self-portrayal.

Thulin gives some very good advice to guide us in the proper use of personal story. First of all, we tell stories to put God in a favorable light and not to put ourselves in a favorable

98

light! Our first person narrative may show our own struggles of faith. Our story, however, does not end with our struggle and rebellion but with God's grace for sinners. We tell the story of our own struggles in order to throw a favorable light on God's gracious love.

A second guideline proposed by Thulin is that the focus of our story be on our experience of God's grace rather than being focused on our experience in and of itself. Our story should never stand alone. It is always a story within the greater story of God's way of salvation. "The preacher's tale is always and only a part of this living tradition."[12]

In the early 1980s the Lutheran Church in America (now a part of the Evangelical Lutheran Church in America) held a series of preaching workshops around the country. These workshops were called: "Preaching From Commitment." Commitment in the title referred to the faith life of the preacher. One aspect of our preaching is that we preach from our own faith commitment.

These seminars proposed a simple approach to the task of preaching. The sermon begins with my story. I tell something out of my own life of faith in relation to the text of scripture. Next comes our story. In this second part of the sermon the point is made that the preacher's story is typical of the stories of all believers. Finally, we tell God's story. The focus of the sermon is on the way that the event of God as told in the text for the day intersects our life and catches us up in the greater story of the reign of God. This approach to the task of sermon construction is a simple and helpful approach. It makes use of "my story" in a larger context of proclamation.

Self-portrayal is a legitimate source of stories for preaching. As we learn to think in story we will often review our own life for appropriate stories to tell. We tell them in order to put God and God's great love for us in a favorable light!

3. Stories Of People And Communities Of Faith

A third source of stories is the stories from the lives of other people and other groups of people. Parish pastors brush up against these stories of faith every day in the normal routine of parish life. These stories of sinner/saints can be wonderful metaphors of participation through which the salvation that is ours in Christ Jesus comes into the lives of our listeners. A very helpful book on this topic has been written by F. Dean Lueking, a Lutheran pastor in River Forest, Illinois. His book is titled: *Preaching: The Art of Connecting God and People.*[13] He describes the aim of the book as follows: "... to help the preacher see the incomparable wealth of meaning that is found in the congregation itself and in the community beyond. It seeks to demonstrate the art of weaving that personal richness into sermons."[14] Lueking seeks to incorporate people of faith into the preached word. Theologically, Lueking affirms, the God of Jesus becomes incarnate within our world and within the lives of specific people. An incarnate God needs incarnate stories to bear witness to God's revealing presence.

Throughout the course of his work Lueking sets forth some practical advice on using the stories of others. Other guidelines come to us from common sense. We won't use the story of a person in our congregation without getting their permission. Sometimes time must pass before a story can be told. Some stories will need to be camouflaged so that the people in the story stay anonymous. Some stories involve issues that do not belong in the pulpit.

In his own parish Lueking will at times have the person tell his/her own story as a part of the sermon. He claims to have found this practice to be particulary useful with senior saints who have gained much wisdom in living out their life of faith. Some churches make use of celebrities to tell such stories. Lueking is convinced that the stories of ordinary people will better represent the cross shaped form of Christian life.

Lueking's book is a joy to read. One quickly realizes that it is a book filled with pastoral wisdom written by a marvelous parish pastor. He does set forth a couple of warning signals about using the stories of people in preaching. He hopes that telling such stories will not be a substitute for serious struggle with the text. He also reminds us that the use of such stories has one primary purpose: as a means of proclaiming the gospel message.

I would add another word of caution. Stories of individuals will almost always deal with individual kinds of problems. Stories of individuals will portray the way God acts in solitary lives. Individually speaking, these kinds of stories have great relevance for us. We want to know how God has worked in other human lives in times of illness, stress, an uncertain future, grief and so forth. We all face these crises of life. We are comforted by the stories of individuals in whose lives God's presence has been revealed.

But not all the problems of the world are individual problems. There are corporate problems as well. Communities of Christian people may find themselves in situations of injustice, oppression, persecution, tyranny and so forth. We need to hear stories of the way God's people have walked through these crises.

The Bible is full of such stories, stories that communities of Christian people in need hold dear. The Israelite people began their days in bondage in Egypt. Jesus had to be taken into Egypt by his parents because of the persecution of male children in the land. The early church suffered great persecution from Roman rule. Oppressed people want to hear these stories over and over again. They rejoice to see how God walks with peoples through their times of strife.

We live out our lives in the church today in America in a land whose values diverge ever more widely from the biblical world of values. How can the church survive in this culture? How can we avoid selling our soul for a pot of gold? Is the church doomed? As preachers we can tell stories of communities of Christian people who have withstood the oppression of their culture. We can tell stories of the African American church in this country or the church in Ethiopia, India, El Salvador, Japan and in many other places where communities of Christian people have steadfastly clung to their faith in spite of living in inhospitable cultures! Communities of faith have persevered in many places through fiery trials.

We need to hear these stories in order to survive as a community of faith in our culture.

4. Stories From The World Of The Arts

A fourth source of stories for the telling is stories taken from the world of the arts. Novels, movies, drama, popular songs and television provide us with wonderful stories for the retelling.

In order to use these stories from the culture a few notes on a "theology of culture" might be in order. Is it legitimate to use stories from the world of the arts in our sermons? My own thinking on this matter is shaped very much by Paul Tillich's theology of culture. Tillich's famous dictum on the matter goes like this: "... religion is the substance of culture and culture is the form of religion."[15]

Religion is the substance of culture. Tillich believed that all humans have their life from the same ground which he often called the "ground of being." All humans are ontologically grounded in God. It is out of this fundamental groundedness in God that humans produce their cultural works of art. Works of art are expressions of a religious grounding. Works of art are ways in which humans seek to come to terms with the ontological reality of their being. Hence, religion is the substance of culture.

Culture is the form of religion. Cultural works of art come forth from the religious grounding of people. Cultural creations, therefore, are the forms in which religious expression takes place. Expressions of culture reveal to us the nature of religion in our time. Tillich believed that every cultural creation expressed an ultimate concern. Ultimate concern is Tillich's way of talking about the human search for its ultimate grounding. Theologians, and that includes pastors, who study culture ought to be able to see the unconscious theological character of the form of religion that is being expressed.

This does not mean that we will find Jesus Christ in the works of human culture. Tillich understands that human beings are sinful. We are estranged from God. Because of our estrangement from God, the works of culture we produce will not be able to give the answers to the human predicament. The answer must be revealed to us through Jesus the Christ. Works of culture give expression to the questions of human existence. This is their great usefulness to the theological enterprise.

Cultural works of art give shape to the questions of life. There is no better place for us to look to find the questions that people are raising than cultural works of art. In law/gospel language I like to say that our artists are the best law preachers we have. Artists do a brilliant job of laying bare the human condition. Popular works of art are popular for a good reason! They give voice to a human malady of the soul that is felt by many people. If we use these works of art in our preaching in order to define the human dilemma we can almost be guaranteed that the picture we paint will be a picture that is relevant to our congregation.

The task of preaching in relation to works of culture is much the same as the task of theology as Tillich described it. Tillich's method is called the method of correlation. The method of correlation, ". . . tries to correlate the questions implied in the situation with the answers implied in the message (of the Bible). It does not derive the answers from the questions . . . nor does it elaborate answers without relating them to the questions . . . . It correlates questions and answers, situation and message, human existence and divine manifestation."[16]

I would want to maintain that the task of preaching is very much the same as the task of theology as here defined by Tillich. Preaching brings the gospel of divine revelation in contact with the questions of human need. Preaching brings God's gospel in contact with people who have experienced God's law. Preaching can perform this task very well using the form of religion that the culture supplies. I have had great success in my ministry with sermons flowing out of the questions expressed through forms of human culture. People find such sermons relevant to life and helpful for their faith.

The challenge of using cultural works of art probably hinges most around the ability to turn the metaphor. The great possibility of such preaching lies precisely in the fact that cultural forms of religion state the human predicament in fresh metaphors. Our task of preaching is to make use of that metaphor to describe the human predicament and then be able to turn that metaphor in such a way that it can also be an expression of divine grace.

In Colleen McCullough's *The Thorn Birds*, for example, the "doctrine" of original sin is expressed through the legend of the thorn birds. The thorn bird at some point in its life unknowingly impales itself on a thorn and sings until it dies. Ms. McCullough gives us the summary of the "theological" point of the novel on its last page. "The bird with the thorn in its breast, it follows an immutable law; it is driven by it knows not what to impale itself, and die singing. At the very instant the thorn enters there is no awareness in it of the dying to come; it simply sings and sings until there is not the life left to utter another note. But we, when we put the thorns in our breast, we know. We understand. And still we do it. Still we do it."

The image of the thorn birds is a powerful metaphor for human sin. We are all like thorn birds, plunging thorns in our breast which leads to our death. Having told this story in our sermon we can then "turn the metaphor" so that it gives expression to the gospel. Jesus wore a crown of thorns. In our sermon we can proclaim that it is in this way that Jesus takes our thorns upon himself and bears them to the cross. The "thorn" metaphor, a new image for telling the old, old story, becomes a language for giving expression to both the human predicament and the divine response. Cultural works of art are filled with metaphors which we can use in just this way. I commend them to you. You cannot, of course, stay current in all the contemporary arts. Choose a field in the arts as your area of concentration: movies, novels, plays, popular songs, etc. You will find much material that can find its way into the pulpit!

5. Creative Fiction

A final source of stories for our sermons are those stories which we ourselves write. Sometimes we know what kind of story we want and need to tell but simply cannot find one from any of the sources we have already discussed. So we write our own story. This is a challenging assignment. We are fortunate if we have had a good course in creative writing to get us started. It is not too late to take such a course or to read a book or two on the art of storytelling.

One of the strongest criticisms of using our own stories is that creating such stories is a work of art which very few of us can master. I certainly honor this word of caution. My experience, however, tells me that we humans are almost natural born storytellers. I have been amazed at the way my students in this art have fashioned their stories. We are not creating the final story after all. We are working with the greatest story ever told. Our stories are always subservient to God's story. Our goal is not to dazzle with our storytelling ability but to simply tell a story in service of a text of scripture.

Creative writing stretches our imagination. I would like to recommend two works on the subject of the use of imagination in preaching. I have referred to these works earlier. One is *Imagination of the Heart: New Understandings in Preaching,* by Paul Scott Wilson. The other is *Imagining A Sermon* by Thomas H. Troeger.

In my own preaching I have created many stories in service of the text for the day. I must confess that I always wonder a little if it is legitimate to create my own story for my own purpose in the sermon. People will often ask, "Pastor, was that story true?" I've come across two answers to such questions that strike me as useful. One answer is that the story is true on the inside. Another answer to the question, "Did this story happen?" is simply: "It happens all the time."

Finally, however, I take my lead from Jesus, the great storyteller. Jesus told many parables. He respected the power of the story. More often than not he did not explain his parables. "If you have ears," he would say, "then hear." In

105

Africa this is often called speaking to the "third ear." We can also tell parables for the "third ear."

These then are our basic sources of stories as we learn to "think in story." In learning how to think in this way it will be helpful if you create a file for stories as you find them. Be on the look out for stories! That's one of the things we must learn to do as we seek to think and speak in a new kind of language.

Stories are told in the service of texts! I close this chapter with this refrain. I want to make it unmistakably clear that texts are the reasons for our stories and parables. Our goal is to enable texts of scripture to come alive for people through the re-telling of these stories, through the telling of other biblical stories, through other stories we tell out of our own life, through stories we tell out of the life of others, through stories we tell out of our culture and through the stories and parables which we create for the situation. God bless you in the telling!

In the telling! Stories come to us from the world of orality. When we use them in the pulpit we need to tell them, not read them. Have you ever stopped to think about the fact that church is just about the only place in our culture where we get to read? Stories used in sermons should be told. Some good old fashioned hard memory work is in order. Work on your stories so you can look your audience in the eye and tell them. Good preaching is almost always eyeball to eyeball. Your eyes capture their attention. If you aren't looking at your people the chances are that your people aren't looking at you either. When the eyes of our audience wander, their minds often wander as well.

---

1. Paul Scott Wilson, *Imagination of the Heart: New Understandings in Preaching* (Nashville, Abingdon Press, 1988), p. 147.
2. Richard A. Jensen, *Telling The Story: Variety and Imagination in Preaching* (Minneapolis, Augsburg Publishing, 1980) p. 151.
3. Mark Ellingsen, *The Integrity of Biblical Narrative: Story in Theology and Proclamation* (Minneapolis, Fortress Press, 1990).

4. *Ibid.,* pp. 14, 15.
5. *Ibid.,* pp. 19-20.
6. *Ibid.,* pp. 28-29.
7. Wilson, *op. cit.,* p. 60.
8. Gustaf Wingren, *The Living Word* (London: SCM, 1960), p. 46.
9. Thomas E. Boomershine, *Story Journey: An Invitation to the Gospel as Storytelling* (Nashville, Abingdon Press, 1988).
10. Richard L. Thulin, *The "I" Of The Sermon* (Minneapolis, Fortress Press 1989).
11. *Ibid.,* p. 76.
12. *Ibid.,* p. 50.
13. F. Dean Lueking, *Preaching: The Art of Connecting God and People* (Waco, Word Books, 1985).
14. *Ibid.,* p. 9.
15. Paul Tillich, *Systematic Theology,* Vol. III (Chicago, The University of Chicago Press, 1963), p. 248.
16. Paul Tillich, *Systematic Theology,* Vol. I (Chicago, The University of Chicago Press, 1951), p. 8.

CHAPTER FIVE
Stitching Stories

I have sought to lay out for you the kind of paradigm shift that I think is necessary for preaching in this post-literate age. That paradigm shift is a shift from "thinking in ideas" in terms of sermon preparation to "thinking in story." Now we must put the nuts and bolts together. How are sermons constructed when we think in story? How are sermons conducted when we understand that many of the characteristics of preaching in an oral culture might be relevant in today's electronic environment? The task of this chapter is to examine these questions.

I want to begin by reviewing the characteristics that I proposed for preaching in an oral culture and making specific comments on each item in terms of sermon preparation.

1. Stitching Stories Together

When I was a student in seminary in the late '50s I was taught homiletics as a "thinking in idea" discipline. I learned to study the text in order to find the ideas. Once I had the idea or ideas of the text clearly in mind the sermon took shape rather quickly. My three points were my three ideas. I then figured out the best way possible to deliver these points/ideas in a way that would help my listener understand what this biblical text was all about. My homiletical instruction, that is, taught me to think in ideas. What ideas are in this text? What ideas can I share with the congregation?

In chapter three I explored some basic starting points for a theology of preaching. I have sought to make it crystal clear that I do not believe that the Bible is primarily a book of ideas. Martin Luther has urged upon us that the Bible should be seen as a means of grace; a means through which Jesus Christ comes to touch and shape our lives. When I now study texts in broader context I look for the realities of the gospel that take hold of my life. When I pause before a text to let it do me good I am looking for a sense of participation in the gospel which I may pass along to my hearers. I have simply found that this is oftentimes best done through stories. Once I have a sense of participation in the gospel message of a text of scripture I look for stories to tell in order that my hearers might also participate in the reality of God's grace.

What stories can I tell? That is the fundamental question that people who "think in story" ask themselves about the text each week. What stories can I tell to enable the gospel reality of the text to become a reality in the lives of the congregation? What stories can I tell? That's where "thinking in story" begins each week on the road from text to sermon. As I have indicated earlier, I first ask: What biblical stories can I tell?

What stories can I tell? And how can I tell them? How shall I stitch them together? You will remember that oral storytellers functioned by stitching stories together. They stitched together bits and pieces and whole stories as they rhapsodized their stories for the life of the people. The "authors" of much of our biblical material also stitched together stories in recording the acts of God in human history. Stitching stories together is the structural component of sermon preparation under the heading of "thinking in story." I will, therefore, leave this structural component to the last. We will first look at the other characteristics of preaching in an oral culture and conclude by looking at structural issues in sermon building.

2. Use Of Repetition

Repetition was necessary in an oral culture because people had only their memories to rely on in retelling the story at a later date. Preaching is oral communication. Unless we put an outline of our sermon in the bulletin or on a slide or overhead projector our listeners also have only their memory to rely on. It is very important, therefore, that the central image of our sermon be repeated several times. It may be just a sentence or a paragraph that we repeat. At any rate, the living center of our sermon needs to be a recurring event of sound.

There is a very practical benefit from the use of repetition. When we can decide what phrase, sentence or paragraph will need repetition in our sermon we will assure ourselves that our sermon has a living center. Many sermons falter at just this point. They do not have a center! We are sometimes quite self-conscious about such repetition. Is it really necessary? This is a "literate" question. Repetition is not as necessary in written communication. The reader has eyes which can recover the center of the message. We must constantly remember that preaching is oral, not literate communication. In oral communication repetition of the living center is vital.

When preaching is guided by "thinking in story" it will not be able to cover many realities! I have indicated this by speaking of the living center of the sermon. Literate sermons typically have three points. "Oral" sermons normally stitch stories together around a single living center. As I indicated in chapter three it will be best if this living center takes the form of proclamation! The living center ought most often to be first or second person, present tense language that enables Jesus to speak words of proclamation through us.

3. Situational Vs. Abstraction

Oral communication typically moves from the particular to the universal. It does not begin with a universal statement and then illustrate the universal with particular examples. Oral communication tells particular stories as the way toward a general or universal reality.

Once we have isolated the living center of the text at hand for our sermon we ask: What stories can I tell? What stories can I tell in order that people can participate in this living center? We are not seeking to explain the idea of the text. The gospel is never an idea! The gospel is an event through which God enters our lives in Jesus Christ. We tell stories in order that people can participate in this gospel reality.

4. A Tone Of Conflict

Conflict was an essential part of oral storytelling. The stories of our group were told over and against the stories of their group. Biblical stories relate the ways in which God won the conflict with chaos, with the Egyptians, with the nations that led them into exile, with Rome, with the principalities and powers of this present world to name just a few. God in Jesus Christ joins the conflict with all the powers that suppress life; with all the powers that deal in death. One of the church's pictures of Christ's atoning work is the picture of Christ the Victor! Preaching does not intend to explain what Christ the Victor means! Preaching intends, rather, to tell stories of Christ's victorious work in such a way that those who hear these stories participate in the victory for themselves!

Eugene Lowry deals with this tone of conflict in a different way in his early work, *The Homiletical Plot: The Sermon as Narrative Art Form.*[1] As the title suggests, Lowry is not so much interested in the flow of ideas as in the plot of a story. He particularly likes stories that function the way most television stories work. Television stories typically begin with a felt discrepancy which then moves to a known conclusion. What we don't know as viewers is how the conclusion, where the heroes of the weekly series will win out after all, is to come about. Lowry believes this kind of plot is amendable for preaching purposes. This is so because those who listen to a sermon also know that the dilemma in a sermon will get worked out in the end. That's why they come to church! They listen intently to the sermon, however, to discover again how it is that God resolves the issue at hand.

Lowry works for tension in the sermon structure. I believe that his understanding of tension is similar to the "tone of conflict" I suggest. According to Lowry, sermons should begin with an upsetting of the equilibrium of the listener. "The central task of any sermon, therefore, is the resolution of that particular central ambiguity."[2] Good things will happen in a sermon where people identify with stories which upset equilibrium and then participate in God's resolution of the imbalance in life.

112

5. Right Brain Communication

Literate training teaches us to organize our sermon in a logical series of ideas. The sermon outline with its points 1, 2 and 3 and perhaps its a, b, c subpoints is a left-brain way of organizing ideas. By that I don't mean to imply that such organization is bad. Identifying such organization as "literate" simply helps us to see that we could structure our sermon in quite different ways.

The metaphor that comes to my mind for right-brain sermon organization is the stitching together of a quilt. Individual pieces and stories are put together to form a whole. And the whole is more than the sum of the individual stories. The whole has a pattern of its own. I would urge you in your story stitching to imagine your sermon as a whole. What kind of pattern are you creating?

6. Metaphors Of Participation

It is absolutely vital for dynamic preaching that we can come to a clear understanding of the difference between metaphors of participation and metaphors of illustration. We begin our task of sermon construction by asking what stories we can tell. We seek to tell stories in which people will participate. The story works by involving people in its reality. At times we will say a few words about the story after we have told it. Our own explanatory words come after the story. Hopefully we won't need to say much. Sometimes we may need to say nothing in terms of application. We simply let the story do its work.

We let the story work because the reality we are seeking to bring alive is something more than idea. Through the stories we tell we are seeking to make the gospel happen in human lives. This is a very different goal from one that seeks to explain the gospel. When we explain we usually begin with the idea and then give an illustration to help people grasp the idea. This is metaphor as illustration. I am convinced that metaphors of illustration do not serve the living gospel of our Lord Jesus Christ as well as metaphors of participation. We ought to seek to tell stories through which the realities of the text become the realities of the hearer.

7. *Thinking In Story*

Our task is to learn a new way of thinking. Please note that storytelling is a way of thinking. It is not that we tell stories in order to do something other than think. Literate culture taught Western Civilization a narrow way of thought. Literate culture taught us to think in ideas as the highest form of human thought. There is certainly nothing wrong with thinking in ideas. But there are other ways to think. One can also think in story. That takes thinking, too, but it works in a different way. I would like to invite you to seek to learn this new way of thinking as one of the ways in which you put sermons together.

The Sermon Is The Story

Having been reminded of the characteristics of preaching in an oral era that may inform our preaching today, let us take a look at the practical ways in which we can stitch stories together. I want to remind you of a related approach to preaching. In *Telling The Story*, I advocated a kind of storytelling where the story is the sermon itself.[3] The sermon, that is, consists of one story with no explanation given. I compared story preaching to the work of the artist. At the end of a novel or movie or play the author does not come out and tell us what it meant! These words of art are open-ended. This open-endedness invites the audience to participate in the completion of the work of art in their own lives.

Preaching can be like that as well. We tell one story that is in a living relationship to the text at hand. The approach that works best is probably a telling of the story in such a way that it lands you in the text in a new way. The story invites you into the text from a different perspective. Our participation in the story leads us to a new form of participation in the text itself. Hopefully the Holy Spirit will be at work in this participation leading the listener to his or her own way of appropriating this text of scripture.

The most powerful possibility of this approach is that the listener makes the connection between the story, the text and his or her own life story. The listener makes the connection! That is much more powerful in the long run than the connections we might make for them.

The down side of story preaching is that the listener might get nothing at all out of the juxtaposition between story and text. That's a real possibility. Hopefully the listener who doesn't get it will talk with others after the service about the sermon. The listener may want to talk with the pastor directly to get it ironed out. I don't see this as a problem. I preached a sermon in a seminary community where the story was the preaching itself. It was truly open-ended. It was a story about a pastor who did not know what he was going to preach on for the next Sunday. The text didn't speak to him. In telling the context of the pastor's life that week I suddenly said that the pastor now knew just what she would say. "Amen," I said and sat down.

Two days later a very bright student came to my office to tell me that this form of preaching didn't work. He and another excellent student, he told me, had discussed the text for two hours the day before and could not agree on what my open-endedness meant. "Let me get this straight," I said. "I preached a sermon on this text which led you and your friend to have a two-hour discussion of the text and I failed?"

In story preaching the preacher is not in total control of the meaning of the text for the congregation. Is that bad? I don't think so! If we have faithfully made the biblical story live we expect that the Holy Spirit will work with this word! The Holy Spirit can enable people to see things through our story that speak to them far more relevantly than we could ever speak. I've experienced this in my own preaching many times. It is important, however, in story preaching that the congregation knows that it might need to discuss the sermon with others later in the day. Story preaching needs that kind of context. I do not consider it a failure when our story preaching triggers extended conversations between parishioners on the text for the day. I have not used this form of preaching very often on my radio broadcasts, however, precisely because I cannot presume that my hearers have a context in which the sermon can receive further discussion.

Before moving on to the matter of sermon construction I am including an example of a "story" sermon that I have used in my radio ministry. It is titled: "Mr. North's Surprise" and is based on Mark 2:15-17. The text appears only at the close of the sermon.

Mr. North's Surprise:
A Story Sermon
(A sermon preached on Lutheran
Vespers on February 12, 1989.)

"The meeting will please come to order," Justin North called out in a strong voice. Justin North was the chair of the church council at Trinity Church. He had held that position longer than anyone in the history of Trinity. Justin North was what you might regard as a pillar of the congregation. Everyone who knew him sensed that he was a devout and dedicated Christian gentleman. His religious convictions ran very deep.

The meeting did come to order. Justin North, as was his custom, led the meeting with prayer. His prayers were usually pretty long. He knew the members of the council quite well. He prayed for several of them by name for specific needs. He asked God's guidance on their deliberations. "Thy will be done," he finally concluded. That was the signature of a Justin North prayer. "Thy will be done."

The first item for discussion that evening was the proposed budget for the next year. The budget committee made their presentation. They had obviously studied the needs of the congregation very thoroughly. They had listened to the membership. Their attention to the concerns of people had caused them to raise spending in a number of the congregation's programs. They intended to make up for that by slashing the mission budget of the congregation. After listening to the discussion for a while Justin North blew his top. "Show me somewhere in the Bible," he shouted, "where we are commanded to take care of ourselves first! It's nowhere! It can't be found. If we need to spend money at home then let's put on a good steward-ship campaign to raise the level of giving. But we can't cut our mission. Mission is who we are!"

The council members were swayed by Mr. North's speech. The mission budget was not cut. Justin heaved a sign of relief and went on to the next item on the agenda. There was a vacancy on the council that had to be filled. The nominating committee recommended Taylor Martin for the vacancy. "Any discussion?" Justin North asked. There was none. "Well, I've got something to say," he continued. "I'm strongly opposed to this nomination. I can't believe you would nominate Taylor Martin for this position. I mean, I can't believe it. He's an alcoholic, folks. An alcoholic! I know he's been dry for a while now. I know he's going to AA. But that doesn't erase the past. What kind of example do we hold up before our members, especially the young people, if we put someone like him on the council. It's as if we approve of his past behavior. We can't do that. His behavior can't be approved. We can't send that kind of message to our members. As church council members we are called upon to live exemplary lives; to set an example for our people. Taylor Martin is not qualified for membership on the council. Putting him on our church council is surely not the way to do God's will. If you approve of this nomination than I will seriously consider resigning from the council in protest." Justin North was a powerful man at Trinity Church. The council voted not to accept the recommendation of the nominating committee.

It was not just on the church council that Justin North demanded excellence. Justin expressed similar views on the school board of which he had been a member for the last eight years. The school board was presently locked in controversy over the high school principal: Phyllis Scribner. Some board members were convinced that she had been using school funds for her own personal use. The evidence seemed pretty conclusive. The complaint of the teachers was that Ms. Scribner didn't deal straight with them. You couldn't trust her word. One day she'd say one thing. The next day she'd say something else. Phyllis Scribner seemed to lack a sense of basic integrity.

The school board decided that one of their members should confront Ms. Scribner personally with the allegations that were piling up against her. Justin North was selected as the board's emissary. So it was that Mr. North came to the high school on Tuesday afternoon. He was ushered in to Ms. Scribner's office. They exchanged small talk for a few minutes and then Justin North launched into the matter at hand. Mr. North had a way of getting to a subject directly. "Now, Ms. Scribner," he began, "I'm sure you are aware of the allegations that have come before the school board. Let's look at the fiscal matter first. We've got some pretty solid evidence that you have been spending school board dollars for your own personal use. Tom Briggs, our treasurer, has the specifics. His most direct allegation is that you bought a new car this past year using money from the transportation budget. His evidence is rather overwhelming. What do you have to say for yourself in this matter?"

"I have nothing to say for myself," Ms. Scribner replied in an aloof tone. "I can't believe these allegations. I won't dignify them with a reply. The burden of proof in this matter rests squarely on your shoulders."

"Oh, that won't do for an answer, Ms. Scribner," Justin North responded, "That just won't do. You're the principal of this school. You hold a position of public trust in this community. You've got to establish to this board and to this school district that your behavior is beyond reproach. What about the allegations made by many of the teachers. They, too, challenge your integrity. They say that you are not a trustworthy person. We've got a whole stack of complaints to that effect. What about it? Do you have anything to say on this subject?"

"No," Phyllis Scribner said testily. "I have nothing to say about that either. You have their word against mine. I tell you it's nothing but a pack of lies."

Justin North left his meeting with Phyllis Scribner more convinced than ever that she had to go. He was sure she was guilty — guilty and hiding behind a smokescreen of silence. He dutifully reported his conversation with her to the school board. Additional evidence pointing to Ms. Scribner's lack of integrity was presented. Justin North just sat there getting more and more angry. He couldn't tolerate people like Phyllis Scribner. Finally he spoke. "I think it's high time we ask for Ms. Scribner's resignation," he said forcefully. "The evidence against her is overwhelming. She has no business in our system. She has no business in our community for that matter. A person like that simply poisons the environment for all of us. The time to act is now."

The school board entertained Justin North's motion but tabled it until the next meeting. The evidence they had needed to be thoroughly checked out before they took final action. The day after the school board meeting Justin North stopped to see his pastor at Trinity Church. He was still fuming over the Phyllis Scribner affair. He was to read the gospel lesson at the Sunday Service and he needed to get information on the reading from Pastor Boyle. "Can I see Pastor Boyle?" he inquired of the church secretary.

"Just a minute," she replied, "he's got someone with him. I'll see how long he'll be. She picked up the phone. In a minute she was back to Mr. North. "Pastor Boyle is about finished with his visitor. He said you could come right in."

Justin North did just that — he went right in. He'd been in Pastor Boyle's office many times before. "Good afternoon, Pastor," he said as he entered the office.

The pastor sat at his desk facing the door. A woman sat opposite the pastor with her back to the entrance. "Well, hi, Justin," Pastor Boyle said. "What brings you here?"

"Oh, I just stopped by to get the gospel reading for Sunday," Mr. North replied. "I didn't mean to interrupt or anything. The secretary said I should come in."

119

"No, no," Pastor Boyle answered, "you're not interrupting. Here, I've got the reading all ready and printed out for you." Pastor Boyle handed the paper over to Mr. North. "Mark 2:15-17" it said in bold script across the top of the page. "Say," Pastor Boyle continued, "do you know Phyllis Scribner here? She's the principal of the high school. Oh, that's right, you're on the board aren't you. Well, anyway, we've been talking a little about her church membership. She might join us here at Trinity."

Justin North just about passed out. What on earth was this woman doing at his church, talking with his pastor? She had no business being there he thought to himself. Doesn't Pastor Boyle know about her he wondered in silence. Justin North greeted Ms. Scribner hurriedly, then turned and beat it for the door. "I'll just wait for you out in the hall if it's okay with you," he said to Pastor Boyle. He couldn't wait to get out of that office. He bolted for the door. He sat down out in the hall in a chair that was provided. Justin North just sat there staring into space. He was dumbstruck at the turn of events. He was angry. How could that woman ever think of joining Trinity? And Pastor Boyle? Didn't he know? Hadn't he heard the charges and suspicions regarding Ms. Scribner? What was he doing even letting her into his office?

As he sat in the hall fuming, Justin North noticed the wadded up piece of paper in his hand. It was the paper that Pastor Boyle had given to him. He looked at it all crumpled in his hand. Slowly he uncrumpled it. "Mark 2:15-17" it said across the top. It was next Sunday's gospel reading, of course. Justin North proceeded to read the words before him. With great surprise he read these words:

And as Jesus sat at table in Levi's house, many tax collectors and sinners were sitting with Jesus and his disciples for there were many who followed him. And the scribes of the Pharisees, when they saw that Jesus was eating with sinners and tax collectors, said to Jesus' disciples, "Why does he eat with tax collectors and sinners?"

And when Jesus heard it, he said to them, "Those who are well have no need of a physician, but those who are sick; I came not to call the righteous, but sinners.

Amen.

Sermon Construction

1. Stitching Stories

I have indicated that the art of sermon construction, the art of creating the whole, the quilt of the sermon, begins with the question: What stories can I tell? Our first task, of course, is to study the biblical text using all the tools of exegesis available to us. We need to pay particular attention to the story character of the text when the text is narrative in nature. How does this story function within the larger whole of this book of the Bible? Why is this story told here? How does it connect with the stories around it?

In seeking to answer such questions we should first of all see our text in light of the context and the book from which it comes. Scripture is its own best interpreter. We should move out of this particular book of the Bible for additional insight only when such a move is absolutely necessary. And we move out of the biblical material to theological material from our tradition with the least frequency of all! I remember so well the preaching I did in my first years of ministry. I could convert any text of scripture into a premise of Lutheran theology in no time flat! Needless to say, that is not biblical preaching.

There are many ways of stitching stories together once we have been engaged with the central event of the text. I will give you some practical suggestions for the beginning of this process. Let us suppose that our text is Mark 2:1-11. This is the story of the healing of the paralytic. Jesus speaks two eventful gospel words in this story. When the paralytic is laid at his feet Jesus surprises everyone by saying: "Son, your sins are forgiven." The scribes shouted blasphemy. "Who can forgive sins but God alone?" Jesus' reply was: "Which is easier, to say to the paralytic, 'Your sins are forgiven,' or to say,

121

'Stand up and take your mat and walk?' But so that you may know that the Son of Man has authority on earth to forgive sins — he said to the paralytic — 'I say to you stand up, take your mat and go to your home.' "

Let us suppose that we decide that the central event of this text is Jesus' proclamation of the forgiveness of sins. There are many texts in the gospels where Jesus makes such first person proclamations. Whenever such proclamations appear in the text I believe we should construct our sermon in such a way that we can enable our congregation to hear Jesus' word of promise addressed to them.

What stories can we tell to enable our listeners to participate in the living center of this text? Let me propose two simple ways to accomplish this reality. First of all, we might retell the gospel story reaching a climax with Jesus' words to the paralytic: "Son, your sins are forgiven."

Next we might tell two or three brief stories of people in need of forgiveness in their life. We tell stories, let us say, of Harold and Harriet and their search in life for a word of forgiveness. Then we bring Harold and Harriet to hear the word of Jesus in this text. "Son, daughter, your sins are forgiven." This word of Jesus is spoken to Harold and Harriet.

After we have enabled Harold and Harriet to hear Jesus' word of forgiveness we can do one of two things. On the one hand, we can invite our hearers as people who need forgiveness, to hear this same word from Jesus. We speak Jesus' word to them. "Son, daughter, your sins are forgiven." On the other hand, we might think that our hearers will have participated in the stories of Harold and Harriet in such a way that they have overheard this word as a word addressed to their own life situation.

These same stories of people in need for forgiveness can be stitched together in a different way. We can tell the stories of Harold and Harriet at the outset of the sermon. We can tell them as open-ended stories of people in need. The stories are not resolved. The tension builds. The equilibrium is upset. In conclusion we tell the biblical story where Jesus' word of forgiveness is heard as a word spoken to the paralytic and to the needy persons in the stories we have just told. In this arrangement we have the same dual possibility of concluding our sermon that I discussed in the preceding paragraph.

"How To Preach A Parable"

Eugene Lowry has written a widely used book suggesting four different ways to stitch stories together. The book is titled: *How To Preach A Parable: Designs for Narrative Sermons.* One purpose of his book is to show ways in which sermons might be designed for texts of scripture that are parabolic or narrative in nature. He suggests four designs. For each design possibility a sermon is included which follows the model. The sermons are by noted preachers of our time. Lowry analyzes these sermons step by step to show how the design is carried out.

I choose not to re-invent the wheel at this point! Lowry's suggestions are fine models of ways to stitch stories together. There is no point for me to try to invent categories of my own when his categories are so useful. I will briefly describe each model and refer you to Lowry's book for further detail. In some cases I will include a sermon of my own to illustrate Lowry's models.

1. Running The Story

This is the simplest design. In each design Lowry uses the word "story" as a reference to the biblical story on which the sermon is based. In "running the story" we simply tell the story from the Bible with our own elaborations, amplifications and flourishes. At the end of the story we make whatever application we feel needs to be made. It is possible, of course, to tell the story in such a way that very little application needs to be made at the end of the story. The living center of this type of sermon comes at the end.

I would urge a living center which turns the story into first person announcement of God and or God's Son to the congregation. We might say something like, "What Jesus is saying to you and me this morning through this story is: 'Son, daughter, your sins are forgiven.' " I use this ending as a reference back to the Mark 2:1-11 text which we discussed earlier. The living center of proclamation of most texts can be rephrased in such first person announcements!

As an example of "running the story" I refer you again to the sermon based on Daniel 4 at the end of Chapter Three titled: "The Most High Sovereign." In this sermon I set the context and then re-tell the story of Daniel 4. At the conclusion of the running of the story I seek to apply the story to our contemporary situation.

2. Delaying The Story

In this story stitching form we begin with stories other than the biblical story in order to set the context for the biblical story. This type of story stitching might be thought of as following a law/gospel structure. We begin with a story or stories that portray the human need for God. We then tell the biblical story as a response to this human need. This is a form of Paul Tillich's "method of correlation" which we discussed earlier.

I include for you now a sermon based on Luke 18:18-27 which is an example of delaying the story. Telling the textual story is delayed while I first tell a story about Burt Reynolds. I then briefly tell the story of the rich ruler as a response to the issues raised by the Burt Reynolds interview. The sermon closes with words of proclamation told in a repetitive manner.

Burt Reynolds And The
Question of Identity — Luke 18:18-30
(A sermon preached on Lutheran
Vespers on Sunday, September 1, 1991.)

I never thought I would preach a sermon featuring the Hollywood actor Burt Reynolds. But here it is. Sometime back I read an article in the Chicago *Tribune* by Howard Reich on Reynolds' new stage show. It's a one-man show titled: "An Evening With Burt Reynolds: The Laughs, the Loves, the Lies, the Legends, (Not Necessarily in That Order)." Reynolds has been traveling the country with this show and receiving warm reviews. Burt Reynolds has quite a story to tell. I call it a story of identity. It's a story that leads us into vital questions about ourselves. Who are we anyway? Where does our identity come from?

For a good share of his life Burt Reynolds got his identity from his fame. From 1977 to 1982 he was the No. 1 box office draw in the world. That's fame all right. "It was an incredible, extraordinary experience," Reynolds is quoted as saying. "It's almost impossible to explain what it feels like to be that big in the first place. When you're No. 1 in the world (it means) you go to China and Bali, and you get off a plane, and they know you. And they not only know you . . . you're like a god to them."

"You're like a god!" Interesting statement isn't it? But being like a god is not easy, says Reynolds. "You're going to find yourself so unhappy because, after you're No. 1, there's only one way to go. You can't stay there, so you're going to drop eventually, and you have to prepare yourself for that." But Reynolds found it impossible to prepare for the fall.

"You're like a god." That statement might have a biblical ring in your ears. That was the temptation that the serpent in the Garden of Eden put before Eve. The serpent tried to convince Eve to eat of the forbidden tree. Eve wouldn't do it. "God said we would die if we ate of that tree," Eve scolded. But the tempter wouldn't give up. "You will not die," the tempter said, "For God knows that when you eat of it your eyes will be opened, and you will be like God." Genesis 3:5. You will be like God! That's the most fundamental temptation that faces us as human beings. The 19th century German philosopher Friedrich Nietschze put it this way: "There can not be a god," he said, "for if there were a god I could not stand not to be that god. Therefore god is dead."

125

Burt Reynolds, like Nietschze, wanted to be "god." He found out, however, that being "god" was hard on his body. His body virtually gave out on him. "I was tired, depressed, hyperventilating, fainting all the time," he said. It took a while but his health eventually came back to him. The trouble was, by that time he was out of the loop! Nobody remembered him. When the gods fall, they really fall. No one called him with work. No one stopped to see him. "When you're dropped by everyone the way I was," Reynolds said, "you need an enormous faith in God or Zen or Buddha or whatever. If you don't have something, you're going to go directly to whatever puts you out of this world, whatever pill, whatever you smoke, whatever you can stick in your arm, whatever you can drink."

In the article I read Reynolds does not identify the face of the god he turned to. His description of the fall of the gods, however, is priceless. When the gods fall and there is no other god you do turn to whatever puts you out of this world. Our society is filled to overflowing with such people: people who can't stand themselves any more. People who can't stand who they are. People who are bereft of an identity.

One more word from Burt Reynolds. "There's a saying in the South," he says, "that no man is a man until his father tells him he is .... Well, my father unfortunately didn't tell me until I was 46. So for 46 years I was a little crazy." And listen to this next line. Reynolds says: "I was looking for an adult to put his arms around me and say ... 'You're a grownup; you can start acting differently now.' "

Reynolds' perception is really on target. Identity is something we cannot achieve. Reynolds achieved a famous identity, of course. He was No. 1. He was the best. He was like a god. But he couldn't sustain his achievement. What do you do after you're No. 1? Reynolds put it well, "There's only one way to go." And that's down.

That's true for any sense of identity we achieve. Please note the important word here. That's the word "achieve." Any identity we have to achieve is an identity we cannot sustain.

Burt Reynolds could not sustain his achievement of being No. 1. No one can. No one can sustain an achieved identity as a great preacher, a marvelous cook, a top salesman, a super executive, a top notch homemaker, a great teacher — you fill in the identity that best fits you. What identity have you achieved that you must forever sustain in order to be someone? I can tell you this. You can't sustain it. The day will come when you can no longer be what you have achieved. Then who are you? If you're like Burt Reynolds, you fall to the bottom of the pack.

Newsweek magazine once ran an article that makes exactly this point. It was titled: "Overstressed by Success." The article talked of how terrifying it is to be at the top. The top in this case referred to top executives, chief executive officers of large corporations. In many ways these are the great heroes of a society like ours where great achievement in business is one of the most common goals. Some make it. We envy them. We shouldn't! At least not according to this *Newsweek* article. The article begins by chronicling the fall of a very successful businessman by the name of Rick Chollet. He was a handsome man, happily married and loved by his colleagues. He had turned a small business into a large and very successful business. Rick Chollet had it all. He was at the top. And he committed suicide. He left a note that said: "Please forgive me, but the thought of going through the torture of living is just too much to bear." Rick Chollet had attained great achievements. But he couldn't sustain these achievements. He couldn't sustain his perceived identity as a captain of industry.

People who work with these successful types speak of their "encore anxiety." They fear, that is, that they won't be able to sustain their earlier achievements. They live in dread of exposure. They are afraid they will be found out. So they drive themselves all the more. Achieve and then achieve some more. They are on a treadmill that never stops. That's just about always the way it is when we set out to achieve an identity. I will say it again. There is no identity that we achieve, that

127

we can earn and carve out for ourselves, that can not be taken away from us in an instant when we can no longer sustain our achievement. "Encore anxiety" is the affliction of the whole human race. "Encore anxiety" is the affliction of human beings this side of the fall who think that by our efforts and determination we can "be like god." "Encore anxiety" is the affliction of the human race when we try to create our own identity. That's really what Burt Reynolds had. He had encore anxiety.

One day an overachiever came to see Jesus. He was a ruler. He knew something about achievement. "Good Teacher," he said to Jesus, "what must I do (there's that word!) to inherit eternal life?" The ruler was willing to do anything he had to do to really accomplish something in life. He wanted to accomplish eternal life! He's a very ambitious ruler.

Jesus tested the ruler. "You know the commandments," Jesus said. "Do not commit adultery, Do not kill, Do not steal, Do not bear false witness, Honor your father and mother." The ruler was elated with Jesus' test. "I have kept all these since my youth," he shouted. An overachiever indeed!

Jesus looked at the ruler. "There's just one more thing you have to achieve," Jesus said in effect. That's always the way it is with achievement. There's always one more thing to do. The thing Jesus had in mind for the ruler had to do with his money. "Sell all that you own and distribute the money to the poor, and you will have treasure in heaven; then come, follow me (Luke 18:22)."

At these words the ruler became very sad. He was very rich. He couldn't do what Jesus asked him to do. He couldn't achieve his identity after all. He walked away! Jesus' disciples observed this scene. They were stunned. This ruler was a wonderful man. He had achieved much. He kept the commandments. He was a man of distinction and character. How could Jesus possibly send this man away? "If this man can't be saved," they said to Jesus, "then who can be saved?" Jesus answered: "What is impossible for mortals is possible for God (Luke 18:26-27)."

128

What is impossible for mortals is possible for God. Here is the answer to the question of human identity. The ruler could not do what he had to do. He couldn't achieve salvation. He couldn't achieve his identity before God. Neither can we. Identity is something that human beings cannot achieve. But it can be given to us. We can receive it. God wants to give us the gift of our identity. It's not possible for us to achieve a secure identity. But God can give it to us. With God all things are possible. God can give us what we cannot achieve. We can receive our identity from God.

My friend Fran Burnford told me a wonderful story about her grandson. His name is Adam. He's now six years old. One day Adam and his mother were driving to church. As they were driving Adam said: "I was baptized five years ago in 1985. My Grandma Fran and I think about that a lot." One of the things Grandma Fran does when she sees Adam is to mark the sign of the cross on his forehead to remind him of who he is. The sign of the cross was made on Adam's forehead when he was baptized. "Adam, child of God, you have been sealed by the Holy Spirit and marked with the cross of Christ forever." That's what the pastor said when Adam was baptized. Adam knows that. When he draws pictures of himself to send to Grandma Fran he puts a cross on his forehead. Adam knows who he is. He knows himself to be a child of God. He has received his identity from God. He has an identity that no power in heaven or hell can take away from him.

Adam knows who he is. Hopefully he will remember who he is when he grows up. If he does he will be spared from having to build an identity for himself. Adam doesn't have to achieve an identity for himself. God gave him an identity as a child of God through the ministry of Jesus Christ.

Burt Reynolds himself hinted at the solution to the identity question when he talked about his father. "There's a saying in the South," Reynolds said, "that no man is a man until his father tells him he is .... I was looking for an adult to put his arms around me." What a wonderful metaphor for baptism. Baptism is one of the places in life where we experience God putting God's arms around us and saying; "You're my son; you're my daughter."

God in Jesus Christ gives us the best identity we could ever ask for. We are God's sons. We are God's daughters. We belong to God. We receive from God an identity that is eternal. And it's all free. Nothing to achieve here. Nothing that can be taken away. Jesus simply says to us from God: "You are my son. You are my daughter."

There is no identity on earth that we can achieve and sustain. The only identity that lasts is the identity we receive from God as a gift.

Jesus says to each of us today: "Don't be like Burt Reynolds or the rich young ruler. Don't count on what you can do to achieve your status in life. It's impossible for you to create your own status. With mortals this is impossible. But what is impossible for you is possible for me. I call you son of God. I call you daughter of God. I invite you to receive from me an identity that lasts forever." Amen.

3. Suspending The Story

This form begins just as the "running the story" model with the retelling of the biblical story. In telling the biblical story, however, we encounter a difficulty. Using the Mark 2:1-11 text again let's suppose that as we retell the story we realize that something more needs to be said about blasphemy. Why did the scribes think Jesus was blaspheming God? We feel this need of further clarification so we "suspend" the story of the text for a moment in order to "explain" the nature of blasphemy in its biblical context. Usually such explanation can also be done in story form.

This form, therefore, begins with the biblical story; suspends that story in order to tell another story or stories to help the story along; returns to the biblical story and finally makes an application to life. This form is similar enough to "delaying" the story that I have chosen to give no sermonic example of the model.

Alternating the Story

This form is designed to move back and forth from the biblical story to our contemporary world. One hears this form often used by preachers in the African-American tradition. One can either begin with the biblical story or with contemporary reality. If, for example, we begin with the biblical story we will suspend this story as we pause to apply the reality of the story to our lives. We return to the biblical story, pause again for application and so on.

My initial reaction to this form was that it would be very difficult to manage. When I look at this form from the perspective of an audience that is electronically massaged by television, however, I see real possibilities. Television programs that are stories may be said to "alternate" the story. We watch a few minutes of one part of the story line, switch to another story, then to a third story, back to the first story and so on. This kind of story alternation is very much part of the experience of our listeners. Alternating the story, therefore, may be a very relevant way of dealing with biblical stories.

I would urge you to consider this form of stitching stories together when you give talks beyond the confines of Sunday morning. I am thinking here of talks you may give in the community, at the school, at a father-son or mother-daughter dinner and so forth. Set as your goal that you are going to tell one bible story that you wish them to know and remember. In the telling of the biblical story you can alternate with real life and say those things you wish to say to this particular audience. Tuck your points inside the story rather than telling stories to illustrate your points. I have experimented with this form in talks to groups of women and men. I used the Book of Ruth for the women's talk and the story of Cain for the talk to men. The response was very favorable.

These are a few suggestions for stitching your stories together. There are many more ways that this can be done. You will discover them as you go. I hope these suggestions, however, can help you begin the process of "thinking in story."

I close this chapter with a Pentecost sermon in which the textual story is told as the frame of the sermon. In the course of the Pentecost story I pause ("alternate") in order to make some more didactic points about the nature and work of the

Holy Spirit. The sermon closes with a series of paragraphs with a repetitive structure that seeks to bring the work of the Holy Spirit to the life of the hearer in a proclamatory fashion.

I Promise Pentecost For You
Acts 2:1-42
*(A sermon preached on Lutheran
Vespers on January 19, 1992.)*

"We need to feel the presence of the Lord, so blow, Spirit, blow." That's the chorus of a marvelous hymn to the Spirit written by Lutheran composer John Ylvisaker. In the Bible the Spirit of God is often associated with the wind or breath of God. In the beginning of time, when all was darkness and void, God's Spirit blew over the creation to bring life in its wake. We read that in Genesis chapter 1. In Genesis 2 we hear that our first parents were fashioned by God from the dust and brought to life by God's breath. We should not be surprised, therefore, when we realize again that the day of Pentecost, the day God poured out the Holy Spirit through Jesus Christ upon all peoples, begins with the rush of a mighty wind. "Blow, Spirit, blow!"

Jesus' disciples did as he had commanded them. They waited in Jerusalem. They waited for God to baptize them with the Holy Spirit and energize them for God's mission to the ends of the earth. On the Jewish festival of Pentecost the disciples were all together in Jerusalem . . . waiting. Their waiting was not in vain. "Suddenly from heaven there came a sound like the rush of a violent wind . . . (Acts 2:2)." The disciples knew that sound. They knew the sound of the Spirit. Wind was the sound of God's Spirit. The wind, the sound of God, filled the whole room. As they looked around the room they could see tongues as of fire dancing over each one's head. "All of them were filled with the Holy Spirit and began to speak in other languages, as the Spirit gave them ability (Acts 2:4)."

This is the most important story in all of the Bible, perhaps, in helping us to grasp and be grasped by the Holy Spirit. Note first where the Spirit comes from. The Holy Spirit comes from outside the room in which the disciples gathered. The Holy Spirit comes from outside of themselves. The Holy Spirit comes from the outside, the Holy Spirit comes from God. It's very important to grasp this reality. There have been times in the life of the Christian church when people have talked as if the Holy Spirit was something inside ourselves. This is not so. When we long for the presence of the Holy Spirit in our life we are not directed to look inside ourselves. We are directed, rather, to look outside ourselves. As we shall see in this Pentecost story, to receive the Holy Spirit into our lives, we are to look outside of ourselves; we are to look to Jesus Christ.

The first manifestation of the Holy Spirit in the lives of the disciples was a Spirit that empowered them to bear witness to Jesus Christ. Since it was the Jewish festival of Pentecost there were Jewish people gathered in Jerusalem from all parts of the world. These Jewish pilgrims spoke all kinds of different languages. These Jews from all over the world also heard the sound of God. They heard the sound of the wind. They traced its origin. And what did they find? They found some unlettered disciples from Galilee speaking to each one of them, in their own language, and telling about God's deeds of power. You can imagine their shock. "How do you know my language?" they might have asked. The fact was that the disciples did know their language and did proclaim to them the deeds of God made manifest in God's son, Jesus.

The Holy Spirit enabled the disciples to proclaim the name of Jesus to all who were in Jerusalem on that long ago Pentecost day. This event is unique. It is unrepeatable. It only happened once. Never again in the New Testament do we hear of Christian people inspired by the Spirit to speak in the languages of other people. There are several places in the Book of Acts where the Holy Spirit enables people to speak in tongues. Speaking in tongues, however, is understood to be an unintelligible language. The Holy Spirit enabled the disciples

133

on the first Pentecost to bear witness to Jesus in intelligible languages. In the book of Acts the Holy Spirit will enable Christians in other cities to speak in unintelligible languages as a sign of God's Spirit in their lives. Likewise, the gift of speaking in tongues that is manifest so often among us today is almost always speaking in unintelligible sounds. Such tongue speaking is a valid gift of the Holy Spirit. It is not, however, the same experience that the disciples had on Pentecost day. What happened to the disciples that day is unrepeatable.

The Jewish people in Jerusalem on Pentecost day couldn't believe their ears. They witnessed a miracle, but they didn't believe it. Miracles do not necessarily have the power to convert people to faith! That's a reality worth remembering. Indeed, some in the crowd mocked the disciples. They accused them of being drunk.

Peter had had enough of the crowd's derision. He got up to speak. He got up to try to explain what had just occurred among them. He assured the crowd that these men weren't drunk. It was too early in the day for that, he declared. Peter went on to make his first point. Peter's first point was that this whole event they had witnessed was the fulfillment of Old Testament prophecy. The prophet Joel, in the Old Testament, had prophesied that in the last days God would, indeed, pour out the Spirit upon all humankind. "Your sons and your daughters shall prophesy," Joel had said, "Your young men shall see visions, and your old men shall dream dreams. Even upon my slaves, both men and women, in those days I will pour out my Spirit and they shall prophesy (Acts 2:17-18)."

Joel's prophesy has come true! That's Peter's point. In the Old Testament the Spirit of God rested on special people and for a limited period of time. Not so in the days after Jesus Christ. In these days the Spirit of God will be poured out on everyone.

Peter then turns to a second explanation for the Pentecost event. First, it is a fulfillment of prophesy. Second, it is caused by Jesus Christ. I always try to make this point abundantly clear. The day of Pentecost is about the Holy Spirit. But when Peter preaches in explanation of the events of this day his address is not centered on the Holy Spirit. His address, rather, is centered in Jesus. Jesus is the author of Pentecost. That's Peter's message.

Peter addresses the Israelites gathered in Jerusalem on that first Pentecost day and tells them about Jesus. Jesus of Nazareth was attested before you by God with power, wonders and signs. And yet, you crucified and killed this man. But God has raised Jesus from the dead, Peter continues. "This Jesus God raised up, and of that all of us are witnesses. Being therefore exalted at the right hand of God, and having received from the Father the promise of the Spirit, he has poured out this that you both see and hear (Acts 2:32-33)." Do you follow that? The language is a little complicated but the point is simple. Peter is explicitly making the point that Jesus is the author of Pentecost. He, Jesus, has poured out this that you both see and hear. Jesus is the One who pours out the Spirit.

Peter's point is as true now as it has ever been. Christian people know that they are supposed to have the Holy Spirit in some way. The New Testament promises the Holy Spirit to believers. But we do not receive the Holy Spirit by talking to, or praying to, or devoting ourselves to the Holy Spirit. The Holy Spirit cannot give you the Holy Spirit! Only Jesus can give you the Holy Spirit. Jesus is the author of Pentecost. Jesus is the one who pours out the Spirit on all believers. If you want to have the Holy Spirit in your life, do what the disciples did. Wait. They waited in Jerusalem. We wait wherever Jesus' story is told among us. When we hear the story of Jesus, or read the story of Jesus, or celebrate the story of Jesus in baptism and the Lord's supper, we are just where we need to be in order to receive the Holy Spirit.

The story of the first Pentecost ends with the response of the crowd to Peter's sermon. I said earlier that what happened to the disciples on the day of Pentecost was an unrepeatable event. What happened to the disciples on the day of Pentecost is different from what happens to us. Our entry into the Pentecost experience is with the crowd. What happens with the crowd is most definitely a repeatable event. The crowd

135

was cut to the heart when they heard that they were responsible for Jesus' death. That's not just true for some Jewish people in New Testament days, however. We are also responsible for Jesus' death. He died for us, remember! And so the crowd asked, and so we might ask, "What should we do (Acts 2:37)?"

And Peter said to them, and Peter says to us: "Repent, and be baptized every one of you in the name of Jesus Christ so that your sins may be forgiven; and you will receive the gift of the Holy Spirit (Acts 2:38)."

On that first Pentecost day 3,000 persons were baptized into the name of Jesus in order that they might receive the Holy Spirit. This event marks the birthday of the Christian church. The Christian church was born on Pentecost.

We rightfully call the Christian church a Pentecost church. By Pentecost church I mean a church whose members come from every corner of the known world. My own church, the Evangelical Lutheran Church in America, says this in the language of inclusivity. The ELCA, that is, wants to be an inclusive church. It shares this vision with most Christian denominations. Most Christian churches want to encompass Jew and Gentile, slave and free, women and men, people of every conceivable ethnic origin. That's really the only kind of church that the church of Jesus Christ can be. But I've decided that I'm not going to use the word "inclusive" any longer to describe this kind of church. I'm going to use the word Pentecost. The Christian church, the Evangelical Lutheran Church in America and every other Christian body, are called to be a Pentecost church. We are called by the Spirit of Pentecost to be a body of people who proclaim the message of God's deeds of power in Christ Jesus to every person on the face of this earth. We are called by the Spirit of Pentecost to welcome into our membership any person of any race or color whose life has been touched by Christ Jesus. We are called by the Spirit of Pentecost to be a Pentecost church.

Peter answered the cry of people in every age. When we are confronted with the reality of our own sinfulness, when we are confronted with the reality that we helped put Jesus to death, we wonder what we can do. "What shall we do?" the crowd demanded of Peter. "What shall we do?" we demand of this chief of the disciples. And Peter tells us that we ought to repent and be baptized in the name of the Lord Jesus so that we, too, might receive the gift of the Holy Spirit.

We long to feel the presence of the Lord in our lives. Peter tells us to repent of the directions we are headed with our life and wait upon the story of Jesus. So we wait upon Jesus in our baptism. And Jesus says to us through the water: "I promise Pentecost to you. I promise to come to live in your body so that you might be a new and different person."

We long to feel the presence of the Lord in our lives. We long to experience the gifts of the Holy Spirit that our lives might be directed by God. So we repent and wait upon Jesus at the Lord's supper. And Jesus says to us through the bread and wine: "I promise Pentecost to you. I promise to give you the gifts you need to carry out my ministry in the world."

We long to feel the presence of the Lord in our lives. We long to experience the fruit of the Holy Spirit that our lives might be directed by God. So we repent and wait upon Jesus in the Word of God spoken and read. And Jesus says to us through God's Word: "I promise Pentecost to you. I promise to give you the fruit of the Spirit so that you may love your neighbor as yourself."

"We long to feel the presence of the Lord, so blow, Spirit, blow." Amen.

---

1. Eugene L. Lowry, *The Homiletical Plot: The Sermon As Narrative Art Form,* (Atlanta, John Knox Press, 1980).
2. *Ibid.,* p. 31.
3. Richard A. Jensen, *Telling the Story: Variety and Imagination in Preaching* (Minneapolis, Augsburg Publishing, 1980) Chapter 5 and 6.
4. Eugene L. Lowry, *How To Preach A Parable: Designs For Narrative Sermons* (Nashville, Abingdon Press, 1989).

CHAPTER SIX
Afterword

We are living in an age of communication revolution. This shift from the literate world of print to the post-literate world of electronic communication has deep and far-reaching consequences for the task of preaching. The burden of this book has been to maintain that one of the responses that we as preachers can make to this communication revolution is that we need to learn to think all over again. Many people who are preaching today were trained in the literate world; we were given literate skills for preaching. We were trained to "think in ideas" as we created our literate, three-point sermons. Post-literate preachers, I have maintained, will need to learn how to "think in stories" in the task of sermon construction. Younger pastors who read this material may have had the good fortune of being introduced to some forms of narrative preaching.

"Thinking in story" is one response to the task of preaching in the midst of our communication revolution. It is not the only response! I expect that we will be treated to a goodly number of proposals for post-literate preaching in the years ahead.

Preaching is never preaching in general. Each preacher lives and works and proclaims within a particular environment. Our audiences differ widely from each other. In terms of media consciousness, who are the people who make up your congregation? A small percentage of your congregation will be persons for whom the literate age is still the dominant factor in their life. Sermons crafted according to literate guidelines will work well in such a context.

In certain kinds of situations your congregation might be dominantly oral in their communication skills. This can happen still today in some urban environments, in hidden away parts of rural America and in missionary assignments overseas.

Sermons crafted under the guidelines of oral communication will be most useful in such settings.

Most congregations, however, feature neither dominantly oral nor dominantly literate members. Most of our members will be people who live in two communication worlds. They are literate and electronic (post-literate) at the same time. Sermons to such congregations can move back and forth between "thinking in ideas" and "thinking in story" sermons. Preaching may be best when it is stereophonic; when it can think in a variety of ways.

There are also congregations where the membership is composed of dominantly post-literate people. Young people may already fit this designation. How are we going to keep the attention of a 15-year-old who watches MTV with regularity? Post-literate sermons will almost always suit this audience best.

The form our preaching takes, therefore, depends somewhat on the people to whom we are preaching. It also depends on the nature of the text for the day. "Thinking in story" clearly works best with narrative passages of scripture. Narrative passages are the dominant form of biblical text. The gospels and most of the Old Testament are presented in narrative form. The epistles are the most significant exception to the rule. The epistles are literary expressions (letters) written by literate authors. They are strongly didactic in nature. Sermons based on the Epistles will quite naturally become literate, didactic sermons. There is nothing wrong with teaching! It is only when teaching becomes the steady diet of the pulpit that it is problematic. It is problematic not only in terms of communication issues. More significantly, didactic preaching is theologically problematic when it is the dominant form of preaching. A steady diet of didactic sermons would mean that the congregation receives the word of good news of God's love in Jesus Christ primarily as information to be learned and understood. Preaching must be able to reach beyond this "information gospel" and learn to proclaim and announce good news. Our hearers need the help of the gospel; not information about help!

Epistle texts are primarily didactic in nature. That does not mean that our entire sermon must of necessity be in the form of a lecture. There are important ways that we can "story" epistle texts. Paul's letters, for example, speak to very concrete situations in life. Our sermons on these texts can spend some time by narrating the story of the people in Corinth or Thessalonica or wherever. Stories can set the context for the words of teaching. Such an approach to an epistle text can make the sermon more interesting and the teaching points more applicable.

Polymorphic Preaching

I have been experimenting with a second approach to the challenge of preaching in a post-literate age. I intend to work on this approach in the years to come. Let me share with you briefly the direction of my thought. In the section on the shape of our electronic communication I indicated that what is sensorially different about our new communication environment is the fact that the dominant medium of television massages many senses simultaneously. The oral world massaged the ear. The literate world massaged the eye. The electronic world can massage both eye and ear at the same time. I called this a polymorphic massage.

My proposal is that preaching can also be polymorphic; preaching can also attempt to massage more than one sense, or one sense from more than one source. I stumbled into this first by accident. I was speaking one Friday night long ago to a youth gathering. These youth were gathered on the floor of a gymnasium. No chairs. Many of them sat with their backs to me. Those who faced me had distractions of their own. Behind me was a balcony. Those youth who were not attending the main meeting were walking back and forth on that balcony behind me grabbing the attention of many of my potential audience. In that context I gave my nicely polished didactic lecture. To this day I'm not sure anyone there heard a word I said.

I was to address this group again the next evening. I knew something had to change. Fortunately for me, there was a

141

clown troupe on the same general program. I got together with the chief clown. We decided to work with the clowns and have them act out, pantomime, my whole talk. Chief clown also suggested we play some music underneath the whole event. We did. It worked like a charm. Now the young people had two things for their ears: my words and the music. They had two things for their eyes: the clowns and me. We engaged the senses of this crowd of young people in such a way that we had their full attention. Polymorphic massage! My message got through to them that night.

I witnessed a similar polymorphism while attending a youth rally in an arena of 15,000 lively teenagers. When the evening began, the program on the stage held the attention of very few of the youth gathered. I was sitting in the balcony. The minds of the youth in that balcony were not on the stage! Then we came to the reading of the scripture. The voice came from off-stage. The lights dimmed. The jazz combo played background music. A dancer moved down a center ramp in rhythm to the music and in sync with the reading. Polymorphic massage! And it worked. The young people sat in rapt attention.

My advice is very simple. If you decide to experiment in this area just think of how you would involve more of the senses of your congregation in the preaching event. A pastor upon hearing me speak of these matters happened upon the text a few weeks later of Jacob's ladder. I spoke with him on the phone later. "Did you try out any of my ideas?" I asked. "Yes," he said, "Last Sunday's text was Jacob's ladder." "You didn't!" I said. "I did!" he replied. And it worked. During the processional hymn a ladder was carried in and set against the back wall. People had something to look at. Their sense of sight was involved. But their wonder was also involved. Why is that ladder there? What is the pastor going to do with it? The parishioners, in other words, were participating in the sermon long before it ever started!

The things you can provide for the eyes of your hearers during the course of your preaching event is only limited by your imagination. Slides, for example, can be a very important tool. You might just flash one or two slides at an important part of your sermon. You might occasionally show a series of fairly fast moving slides at a point in your message. By involving people's eyes more fully you normally attract them more deeply into the event of your sermon.

Perhaps the easiest and most effective sense to add to your sermon is the sense of hearing. The congregation hears you and something else at the same time. That something else might normally be music. Instrumental music can make a wonderful undergirding for parts of your sermon. Oral communities use music as a background for speaking in a very natural way. It may seem at first that it would bother people to have two sounds (music and speech) going at the same time. But listen to the radio or the television! They do it all the time. People are used to it!

Music can be a powerful accompaniment for preaching. Maybe the best way to start is to select a well-known hymn that will be the hymn sung after the sermon. Have the music of that hymn start quietly as you move toward the climax of your sermon. Experiment with a variety of ways of adding music to your preaching. Find what works and what does not work. Each community of hearers, after all, is different. Good luck to you as you practice your own form of polymorphic massage!

What Can Go Wrong?

My fundamental message has been advice to learn to "think in story" as a means of communicating the gospel in this electronic age. I am often asked what the pitfalls are to this approach to preaching. One of the problems is that which I touched on just a few pages ago. Audience makes all the difference in the world! The kinds of approaches I am suggesting for preaching today work best in oral cultures and in cultures where the post-literate electronic massage has had a powerful impact.

143

What can go wrong? Theology can go wrong! Narrative cannot save us from bad theology. We can tell wonderful stories in the service of questionable theology. Storytelling is not a substitute for disciplined study of theology nor for disciplined study of the text for the week. Preaching as storytelling is not intended to be a substitute for hard theological and exegetical work! Preachers are not in the entertainment business! Our goal is not to tell good stories. Our goal is to communicate the biblical story through our use of story.

"Thinking in story" is hard work! We cannot creatively re-present the gospel message in story form if we have not at first understood it very well. "Thinking in story" works imaginatively with what we know of the text before us. Our first task as preachers, therefore, is to be sure that we know the biblical and theological world in as much depth as we can. Such work is indispensable for preaching in any format!

What can go wrong? Our stories can be perceived as ends in themselves. "Isn't she a great storyteller?" people might say in response to our sermons. If that's the basic response to our storied preaching we are in trouble. It is not sufficient that our stories call attention primarily to our brilliance as storytellers. One of the solutions to this problem is that we focus first of all on the biblical story. Tell the Bible's stories. I find that preachers are hesitant to tell the biblical story, even the text for the day. We seem to assume that people know these stories already. Some do. Most don't! Tell them again. I'm sure you know from your own experience that these stories continually speak to us in new ways. They will speak to our hearers in new ways as well. When in doubt, tell Bible stories. Tell today's story in its biblical context. Tell other Bible stories that help listeners to hear the realities of this text in new ways.

What can go wrong? Even the preacher who tells Bible stories can interpret them in such a way that they do little justice to their biblical origin or to Christ's gospel. So we're back where we began. Biblical study. Theological study. All the brilliant advice in the world about preaching, story or other, cannot save us from poor preparation. Good preaching must be grounded in an in-depth understanding of the biblical world. Good preaching must be grounded in an in-depth understanding of our theological traditions. It is of hard work in the study, and hard work in listening to the cries of our people and the world, that good preaching is born. Our hard biblical and theological work will lead us to ever new discoveries of the amazing grace of God for sinful humanity. Grasped by the incredible good news of the story we are to proclaim, we will find the stories to tell.